UK WINE

A BASIC GUIDE FOR CONSUMERS

Picture courtesy of Three Choirs Vinyards

Gateway Books International

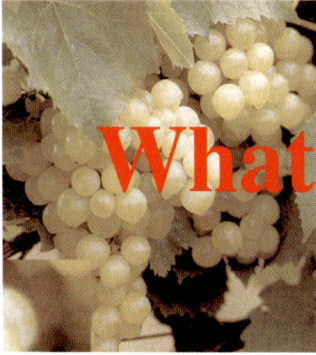

What's Inside

*Front *cover picture courtesy of Chiltern Valley Wines*

© **Gateway Books International**

gbmir@hotmail.com

ISBN 0-921333-85-4

Having sampled a number of UK wines over the years I can safely agree that a good one rivals the best from overseas.

But many people still don't know that wine is made in the UK from vines grown here in vineyards across the sunnier parts of Britain.

And even if they are aware it is often not easy to track down a bottle. As often as not UK wines are stumbled upon at country markets or other chance visits.

The problem, as several contributors note in this guide, is that UK wine is still produced in relatively small quantities and out of a selection of hundreds or even thousands of wines on a retailer's shelf only a handful may be from the UK.

Yet UK wine is on sale at supermarkets, retailers, hotels, restaurants, vineyards, by mail order and through the Internet.

That is why we decided to make this consumer guide: to try to give more people more information about UK wine and where to get it.

If you want to know what grapes are grown in the UK

and what kinds of wine are made, this guide provides the basic details.

Plus there is a selection of vineyards which you can visit around the country with a comprehensive list at the rear which you can use to find vineyards yourself. Tourist information offices can usually help you locate the vineyards.

Some people now include vineyards as part of their holiday itinerary and although only a handful offer bed and breakfast there is virtually always a pleasant rustic pub nearby where you can spend the night after a tasting or two.

That is the delight of vineyard visiting or even vineyard hopping. If you want to, you can have a look round and see how the vines are grown and the wines made. But if you just want to taste and buy some wines you can do that, too. In some areas there are a number of vineyards clustered together so it is practical to visit several.

I hope all of you who read this book will be inspired to find out more about UK wine and I would like to thank most sincerely all those UK wine makers and vineyard owners who have joined me to make this publication.

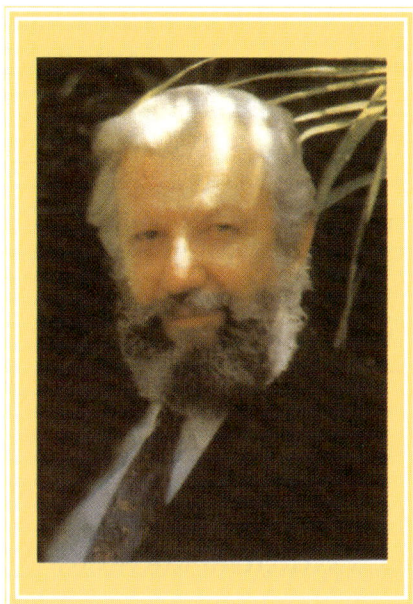

Richard Mann

Good UK Wines Stand Up To Comparison

Stephen Skelton is Chairman of the United Kingdom Vineyards Association, a successful vine grower and wine maker and a well-known writer and lecturer about the UK industry and about wine making. He is the author of the most up-to-date overview of the UK wine industry: ' The Wines Of Britain And Ireland: A Guide To The Vineyards' published by Faber & Faber.

"These days, UK producers pushing wine out into the commercial market have generally applied very good technical standards because this is the only way to compete effectively with wines from all over the world.

Those people who have been most successful have been people able to identify markets in which they are unique, with charisma and willing to get on with promoting their products themselves.

Even though English wine is only a very small part of all wines sold in the UK, consumers should be open to varying their wine 'diet' to include the wines not only of the large suppliers but smaller producers such as the UK. Good UK wines stand up to comparison both in terms of quality and price.

An important recommendation of English wines that appeals to me is that they are lighter than many from overseas with an alcohol content of only 10.5 to 12.5 percent meaning that you can drink them quite comfortably either as an aperitif or with a meal. Two or three glasses of a wine with an alcohol content of between 13.5 to 14.5 percent is just too much to be drunk comfortably. English wines are a very light and pleasant alternative which I think fit in very well with people's eating and drinking habits these days.

UK wines may lack visibility in retail outlets but in the case of supermarkets, for example, I believe they do as much as they can and more to support us. The fact is that many people in the wine retail trade have developed their careers interactively with many of us on the production side and are very well aware of the calibre of English wine.

The basic problem for UK wine is the very small amount of wine being made for the commercial market. For example, First Quench have 3,000 shops while the UK wine industry produces only about one million bottles a year - and that's only one chain including Threshers, Victoria Wine, Haddows, Wine Rack and so on.

On the other hand I wouldn't argue that we necessarily need more vineyards to increase the supply. What I think we need to do is to build on the knowledge and experience of the currently successful people and encourage existing vineyards to produce wine that's as good as the best. The best English wines are without doubt of world standard.

Unfortunately, probably half of UK wine makers could benefit from some improvement in the way they do things - in terms of growing skills, wine making skills and their methods of marketing. There's still a lot to do. It's taken us 50 years to get to the point where we are today.

Fundamentally, growers have to decide why they want to have a vineyard and to face up to the issues involved. Slowly, the pattern developing seems to be that bigger vineyards are relying more and more on grapes brought in from outside meaning that growers will grow

* *Picture courtesy of New Wave Wines*

better and better quality grapes to be able to meet this sort of demand.

Very small growers will sell either to local markets, sell their grapes to somebody else or give up. There isn't much room in the market for a small, undercapitalized grower to sell wine through the major retail outlets. And they don't have the resources or the volume of production on which to base the costs of promotion, marketing or even of labelling.

I have met hundreds of growers who have set up vineyards and wineries for completely the wrong reasons - namely that they fancy the idea of owning a vineyard. The practical problems don't seem to deter them until it gets to the point where the problems overwhelm them and then they have to decide what to do with the vineyard. Human nature being what it is, most people are reluctant to face grubbing up something in which they've invested time and money so they decide to run the vineyard on a shoe string, grow grapes of a dubious standard and have them made into wine as cheaply as they can. The result is that such wine is never the best, they don't have the money to promote it and often such vineyards just gradually decline.

A very good way for smaller producers of good wine to sell their product is to sell it at the vineyard gate where the wine can be sold direct to the public but it helps if you have something other than wine to attract the visitor - a castle, for example, or some other tourist attraction and if that something has a shop attached to it then it's better still. I would advise anybody intending to sell wine at the vineyard gate to at least have a farm shop otherwise even gate sales are going to be very difficult. It's also good if you can sell locally to wine bars, hotels, restaurants or other suitable outlets.

Overall, the number of vineyards is in fact falling while the acreage under vines is increasing so this means that a lot of smaller growers are getting out and larger growers are getting bigger."

Blind tasting at the English Wine Festvial

Where To Find Out About UK Wine

United Kingdom Vineyards Association
 Church Road, Bruisyard, Saxmundham,
 Suffolk, IP17 2EF
 Tel: 01728 638080 Fax: 08701 363708
 E-mail: 106236.463@compuserve.com

President: Lord Montagu of Beaulieu
Chairman: Stephen Skelton: email: spskelton@btinternet.com
Secretary: Peter Farmer, Moorlynch Vineyard, Moorlynch,
Bridgwater, Somerset, TA7 9BU
Treasurer: Roger Marchbank, The Coach House, Salisbury Road,
West Wellow, Romsey, Hants., SO51 6BW
General Secretary: Ian Berwick, UKVA, Church Road,
Bruisyard, Saxmundham, Suffolk, IP17 2EF

For information, please contact: Ian Berwick

Affiliated Regional Associations
These associations represent the vineyards within their designated
regions.

East Anglian Winegrowers Association
(Norfolk, Suffolk, Essex, Cambridgeshire, Bedfordshire,
Hertfordshire, and London North)

Chairman:
Donald Cooper, Fletchers, Fletchers Lane, Middleton,
Saxmundham, Suffolk, IP17 3NZ
Tel: 01728 648471   Fax: 01728 648471
e-mail:HYPERLINK mail to nevards@aol.com

Mercian Vineyards Association
(Cheshire, Leicestershire, Northamptonshire, West Midlands,
Yorkshire, Shropshire, Nottinghamshire, Derbyshire,
Staffordshire, Warwickshire, and Rutland)

Chairman:
George Bowden, Leventhorpe Vineyard, Bullerthorpe
Lane, Woodlesford, Leeds, West Yorkshire, LS26 8AF
Tel: 01132 667892   Fax: 01132 667892
e-mail:HYPERLINK
mailto:george@leventhorpevineyard.freeserve.co.uk

South East Vineyards Association
(Kent, Surrey, East Sussex. West Sussex, and London South)

Chairman:
Samantha Linter, Bookers Vineyard, Foxhole Lane, Bolney,
West Sussex, RH17 5NB
Tel: 01444 881575   Fax: 01444 881399
e-mail: HYPERLINK mailto: sam@bookersvineyard.co.uk

South West Vineyards Association
(Cornwall, Devon, Somerset, Avon, Herefordshire,
Worcestershire, Gloucestershire, and the Counties of Wales)

Chairman:
Peter Farmer, Moorlynch Vineyard, Moorlynch,

Near Bridgwater,
Somerset, TA7 9BU
Tel: 01458 210393   Fax: 01458 210247
e-mail HYPERLINK mailto:moorlynch@aol.com

Thames & Chiltern Vineyards Association
(Berkshire, Buckinghamshire, Oxfordshire, and London West)

Chairman:
Ann Bishop, Bouncers Farm, Wickham Hall Lane,
Wickham Bishops, Witham, Essex, CM8 3JJ
Tel: 01621 89133O
e-mail:HYPERLINK mailto:wrenserenade@aol.com

Wessex Vineyards Association
(Hampshire, Dorset, Wiltshire, and Isle of Wight)

Chairman:
Roger Marchbank, The Coach House, Salisbury Road,
West Wellow, Romsey, Hants., SO51 6BW
Tel: 01794 323345   Fax: 01794 323345
e-mail:HYPERLINK mailto:roger.marchbank@talk21.com

One Of The UK's Best Kept Secrets

By Richard Mann

The mushrooming of wine publications and wine retail outlets attests to the ever increasing popularity of wine in Britain.

But UK wine, meaning wines made in England and Wales, has not often been seen to share in this popularity even though sales have been increasing.

Even people working in pubs or selling wine from other retail outlets close to vineyards often don't know that there is one near by.

The UK is not a land famous for wine growing - unlike France, Germany or Portugal - and English wine has not achieved the kind of brand image established by wines made in parts of Europe.

There are still many people who don't know that wine is made in the UK and what kind of wines are available.

Plus, there remains a consumer attitude similar to the one-time reaction to Australian or Californian wines, namely that English wine can't be any good because it doesn't come from a region famous for making wine.

In fact, there are nearly 400 vineyards of various sizes in the UK producing white, red, rose and sparkling wines. And a wide range of traditional fruit and herb wines continues to be produced. Last year more vines were imported into the UK than ever.

Part of the problem is availability. Wines in the UK are more often than not produced by smaller vineyards which generally do not satisfy supermarkets or wine retail chain's requirements for volume.

As a result, UK wine is most often available only local to the place of being made - it may be sold in the local supermarket branch, the local hotel or pub and in some local shops. Indeed, some vineyards manage to supply dozens of outlets within a nearby radius and a few sell throughout the nation by means of mail order and even the internet.

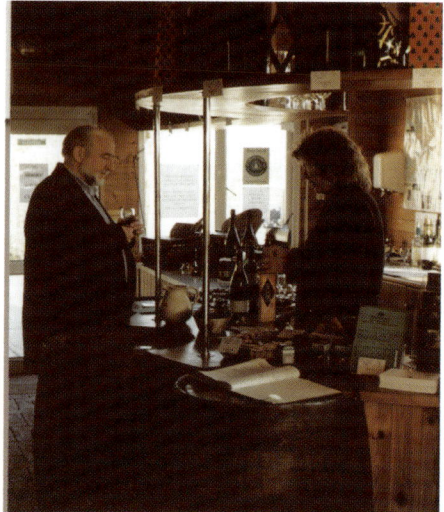

Tasting wine at a vineyard shop

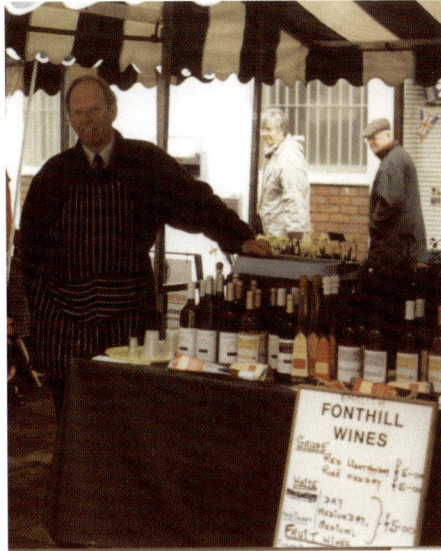

Wines are often sold at farmers' markets. This vendor is at Winchester.

In addition, UK wine is sold at farmers' markets, food festivals and county shows. UK wines are widely available at castles, country homes, restaurants, cafes and supermarkets throughout the grape growing areas of the UK, often close to the point of production.

Some producers supply wines to prestige events such as House of Commons celebrations or events at London's Guildhall while others sell at upmarket stores such as Fortnum & Mason.

Visiting a vineyard can be great fun. There is almost always a tour of the vines and the winery, if there is one on site, culminating in explanations about the wines and tastings. Some vineyards can provide picnic or sit down meals to make the visit a complete day out. And a few provide facilities for bed and breakfast.

Some vineyards lease vines to members of the public so that individuals can enjoy their very own wines, others create personalized labels on wines which can then be given as gifts.

UK vineyards tend to be clustered together in some of the around 10 regions in which vines are grown and wine breaks are quite feasible in which a weekend away may be designed around visiting and staying at or close to vineyards and combining wine with food, good company and a break away combined with seeing the local tourist sights.

Wine is often not the only business of those who grow vines or make wine although there are a handful of very large vineyards and wineries run by world-class wine makers and selling large volumes of wine.

Many of the vineyard owners are colourful characters, well worth meeting in addition to sampling the wine.

The wine trade itself is convinced that the UK produces distinctive wines which can compete with any in the world and to prove it producers enter and do well in a range of regional, national and even international competitions. Such competitions may not mean much to consumers but wine makers are delighted, encouraged and reassured by the accolades they receive.

To try to generate more public awareness about UK wine, the industry has an annual calendar of events including Wine Week at the beginning of June and the Wine Festival in September.

Vineyards and events are routinely promoted in tourist brochures and leaflets and producers say that regional and national media give the industry excellent coverage.

Readers of this guide who want more information can obtain it from the UK Vineyards Association of from the English Wine Producers.

It is also worth knowing that some wine producers give talks about wine in their localities and that there are courses about wine making at a number of centres. Some areas have wine clubs and wine circles and wine tastings are often promoted in the local press.

"The Future For UK Wine Is Bright"

Frazer Thompson,
Managing Director, New Wave Wines Limited

Frazer Thompson believes that the prospects for UK wine are better than ever, despite the fact that some consumers are still in the dark about what wines are produced here and about the quality.

" In the UK, we haven't been making wine for very long, certainly if one was to compare with the French who have been making wine for 2000 years. However, you must bear in mind that while there are people in France who make wonderful wine, the vast majority of French wine is pretty poor but we don't tend to hear about it because it doesn't leave the country. In that sense we've done very well so far.

If you look at the history of English wine it really only got under way seriously in the 1970s with a few mad cap pioneers who decided that they'd have a go at growing grapes in England including David Carr Taylor, Kenneth Macalpine at Lamberhurst and Stephen Skelton at Tenterden. There were others too, of course, and as you'd expect in any new industry some found it hard going because they had no marketing funds and some even went to the wall. Most were small vineyards with no cooperation between them and as a result relatively high costs.

This first wave of vine growers and wine makers was replaced by a second wave of slightly more professional and commercial enterprises. The reality is that there are still too many of these given the size and character of the industry.

What we see with New Wave Wines Limited is effectively the new wave characterized by the consolidation of three of the largest producers, Carr Taylor, Lamberhurst and Chapel Down into New Wave Wines Limited and by far and away the largest wine producers and marketers in the UK accounting for about 50 percent of all commercial wine sales. We're in most major supermarket chains including Waitrose, Tescos, Sainsbury's, Safeways, ASDA, Majestic and Unwins. We sell in excess of 400,000 bottles of wine per annum. Around 150,000 visitors visit our vineyard shops every year.

Many vineyards are not selling into the open market at all but are essentially vineyard gate operations where tourists are attracted to a property and wine is sold as one of several revenue making activities. Their core business may not be selling wine whereas our is. Because it is, we welcome growers discussing their plans with us and discussing prices so that we can work closely together.

How has the English wine scene been helped by foreign winemakers ?

British viticulture has been massively helped by wine makers coming here from overseas, especially from Australia. Any new industry needs help from people who've done it all before. Particularly in the case of sparkling wine, we have had no shame in asking people from Champagne to help us. As the industry develops it is becoming more professional both in terms of wine making and wine marketing.

How can you persuade people to try your wine?

Our industry is embrionic. English wine accounts for only about 0.2 percent of the UK wine market and so it's difficult to find. Also, in the majority of shops, there isn't a category for English wines. Visibility, therefore, is a real problem. The challenge for commercial organizations such as ourselves is to make more 'noise' than our share of 'voice' would normally allow.

When people pay money to buy wine they're not just buying a bottle of wine. What they're really buying is a story. In the same way that a pint of Heineken means different things than a pint of Fosters so when you buy wine you're buying more than just fermented grape juice but a history as well. The stronger the story the stronger the emotional pull of the product, and the more powerful the marketing message. Our experience is that if you present a bottle of English wine without revealing that its English when the secret comes out people's jaws drop. English wine is a great story - different, distinctive, original and British. We know from sampling exercises that once consumers buy English wine they're hooked. People become very loyal to English wine and we have a large number of retained customers. We believe that the future of English wine is very bright.

The issue about English wine is not that its of bad quality but the scale of production. English viticulture is a very small industry and one that includes hobbyists as well as some largish commercial enterprises such as our own. The future reputation of English wine is dependent upon those hobbyists determined to make good quality wine.

How will your marketing be different?

Instead of apologizing for gizing for the climate we have to make wines that are interesting from grapes that grow well in Britain's climate. Grapes that grow well here are

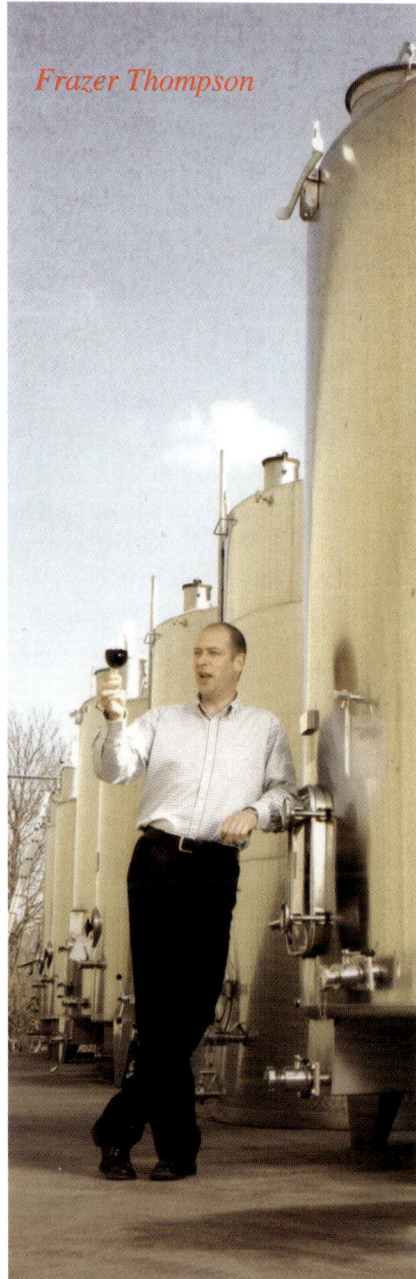

Frazer Thompson

not necessarily ones that people have heard of and, if wine makers want to make a virtue out of the unusual grapes we grow here, they have to face the fact that a differnt style of marketing is required.

For example, there is now a large group of people who call themselves the ABCs - Anything But Chardonnays. To most niche marketing people these people are a dream market to sell to because they are by nature promiscuous in the way that they consume brands. In other words they would be the people who would have arrived at your dinner party twenty years ago clutching a bottle of Australian Shiraz from a country that you never thought could produce decent wine and made from a grape variety you'd never heard of. Now, sure enough, it's turned out to be a great variety. These people are the wine trail blazers, constantly on the look out for the next new thing. But things have changed because instead of being a small group of people the ABCs now constitute a considerable proportion of the population and the sort of people who are responding well to UK wines.

In Britain we have to make a virtue of the fact that our wines are different and distinctive, of high quality and will provide a good and guaranteed taste experience. Instead of apologizing for the grapes we grow we should be up front in saying, for example: "Try Bacchus. It tastes a bit like

Sauvignon Blanc but we think that it's better. It suits England better and we think that Bacchus is a more interesting grape."

It helps buyers these days that many wine bottles bear labels describing the grapes used and the taste. It's essential that we tell people that what goes into English wine is firstly high quality grapes ,secondly the varietals that go into it and finally what taste to expect. Usually well known drinks brands or the reputation of the retailer reassures buyers but, in the case of English wine, producers have to assume some of that responsibility by providing the kind of detail on a label that will reassure the customer.

How is the English wine industry changing?

The industry is at present splitting between those who are great professional grape growers and those who turn those grapes into great wine and are able to package this in a way attractive to the consumer and provide distribution and sales channels.

New Wave Wines PLC buys grapes from a number of different sources but there is only one winery, one centre of excellence. Wine making thus has become a business proposition and not just someone's flight of fancy. One of the things we have to do is to be extremely stringent on quality control because no serious commercial organization can afford to sell even one bottle of bad wine. There are many small producers in the market and I can only hope that the quality of some of their wines is not putting the consumer off English wine.

The message we must get across is that there are English wines of extraordinarily high quality and well worth paying the money consumers are being asked to pay. Our job at New Wave Wines is really to trail blaze and create an English wine brand and I think the entire English wine industry will benefit from this. The more successful we are the more people may decide to open vineyards across the UK thus creating a position which allows us to grow. At the moment all the wines in England are new and innovative and bringing these wines to market is the agenda of New Wave Wines.

What about the future for English wine?

We think that the long term commercial future of English wine is in sparkling wine, in terms of climatology, geology and revenue; it's a fantastic opportunity. Not many people know that the South Island of New Zealand, Champagne and ourselves make the best sparkling wine in the world and share the same geographical advantages.

In the future we'll concentrate on sparkling wine and also on the new and innovative still wines which we're calling 'Curious Grape' a name which very much makes a virtue out of the originality of the wines made in the UK.

There is no constraint on what grapes can be grown in the UK but because we live in a northern temperate climate we have to face that not all grapes are going to yield a commercial crop. The UK is going to be best at producing the kind of grapes grown in other temperate climes such as the South Island of New Zealand, the Rhine area of Germany or Northern France. These are rather acidic grapes producing dry, crisp and rather citric wines with plenty of taste and zest. England can produce these wines in abundance and with very delicate fragrance. At the moment these are becoming the 'flavour of the month' in contrast with the big, fat, high alcohol, buttery, thick, oaked wines. These flavours have their place but there are far more occasions when you want something sharp, will cut through oil and has real taste. What we want to get across is that dry wines like this with very delicate fragrances and aromas are very English in character.

You've just won a hatful of medals for your wines. Does it make a difference?

Many UK wines have now won awards both at home and abroad and while they may not mean much to the consumer such awards are in fact a badge of reassurance. Also, from a manufacturer's point of view, it's good to see how our wines compare and with whose products they compare; an award creates a benchmark and forces quality. If producers are really true to what they're doing rather then just being crassly commercial and trying to turn grape juice into an alcoholic beverage then they have to send their wines away for an independent expert assessment.

You produce in one of the most expensive land areas in the world. Surely you can't compete on price?

The commercial reality of wine production in the UK is that

we cannot realistically sell wine for less than about £4.50 to £5.00 per bottle - the duty alone is £1.16 for still and £1.60 for sparkling and then you've got to bottle, cork and label your wine. This is above the average supermarket price but UK producers are tiny players in a market where the big producers keep prices down by producing millions of gallons of wine. You must remember, too, that land in the UK is relatively scarce and expensive and that wine growers receive no government subsidies, something which I find appalling. In France, for example the industry is massively subsidized by the French government because it realizes the crucial importance of wine to the rural economy.

The reality is that in the UK we produce a very small quantity of very high quality wines. But for £5 to £6 you should get a very good and distinctive wine indeed. We have no interest in keeping prices higher than they should be because we want the wines to be affordable enough for people to want to try them, thus stimulating the UK's wine industry as a whole.

Vine growing makes the countryside look wonderful, employs people in the rural economy and provides an opportunity for fabulous tours. The more success we have in selling UK wines, the more vineyards we will see. I think the main reason for the growing popularity of vineyards is that it represents an alternative use for land - people are always looking for new ways to make money from land and having a vineyards is in any case a beautiful thing. We pay about £500 per ton for grapes or about £2,000 per acre. There are not many other rural industries yielding that sort of return, despite the costs of viticulture.

Grape Growing In A Cool Climate

By Will Davenport

"The flavours and styles of the wines are unrivalled by any overseas producer."

Think about the idyllic vineyard setting and you may en visage rows of vines growing in stony soil, basking in permanent sunshine, probably with a Provence Chateau in the background. This is the vine's traditional territory, and they thrive here, producing bountiful crops of sweet juicy grapes. Then consider the average British summer. Sunshine does feature, but the temperatures are significantly lower and it rains occasionally, sometimes more than occasionally. The vine thrives here too; it is a very adaptable plant. British grape growers are part of the 'very cool climate' group - a club that includes Champagne, Canada, Oregon and parts of New Zealand and Germany.

From a grower's point of view, the cool climate makes the task harder. The variability of the weather always has to be accounted for. The vines produce much smaller crops in cooler conditions, making wine production more expensive. The higher rainfall can lead to an increased risk of mildew and botrytis. Worst of all, a frost in May, or even June, can destroy all the hopes of the most optimistic winemaker when the young emerging shoots wither and turn brown to be replaced by a late second growth. At the other end of the season the autumn weather can be magnificent, or it can be wet and miserable. Nothing can be taken for granted.

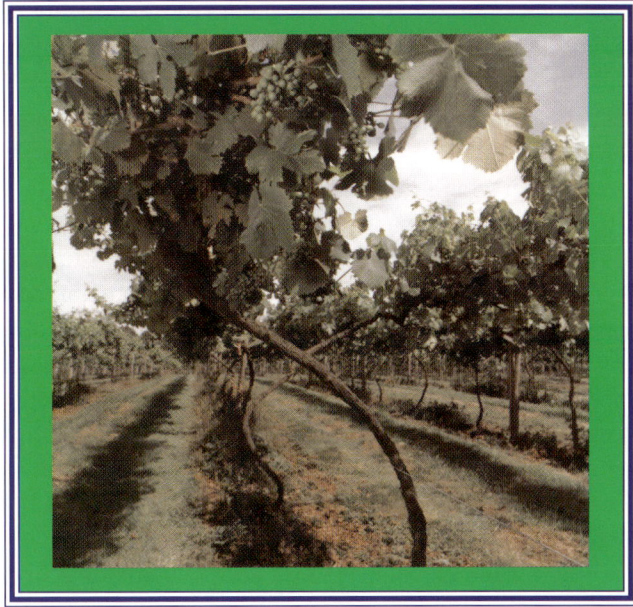

It all sounds so depressing that you may ask why anybody bothers to grow grapes in such an environment. Of all the cool climate regions, Britain is among the most challenging, and is pushing the extremes of possibilities. The available choice of grape varieties is limited by the climate, and so most of the familiar names (Cabernet Sauvignon, Merlot, Shiraz, Semillon, Muscat, Gewurztraminer etc.) will not generally be found in UK vineyards. We have Pinot Noir and Chardonnay, but the mainstay of the industry are our own stars - grape varieties like Reichensteiner, Huxelrebe and Siegerrebe, performing at their peak in the cooler climate, and capable of giving stunning flavours.

However Britain's grape growers are proud members of the 'cool climate club'. Cool climates need intelligent grape growers to ensure success. Many of the cool climate regions are renowned for the high quality of their wines and these are wines with class. We have learnt to make an asset out of our climate. The varieties that are grown give us wines of great distinction, and this is mainly due to the climate that the vines exist in. With careful selection of a good vineyard site, and by choosing grape varieties that are suited to the conditions on that site, grapes can be ripened every year in

England and Wales. The ripe grapes are unlike those grown in any other region of the world, unique to Britain. The flavours and styles of the wines are also unrivalled by any overseas producer. Indeed we have a product that is completely British and entirely created by the soil that we stand on and the climate that we live in.

English wine includes a wide range of styles, from dry white to sparkling, red to dessert wine. Every one of these styles relies on the characteristics of the grapes for their quality. The cooler climate means that the harvest takes place later than most overseas regions, sometimes into November. The grapes form their flavours over a long season and with careful winemaking these flavours can produce the most exquisitely perfumed white wines. Grape varieties such as Bacchus, Schonburger and Ortega may not be household names, but they produce wines that are delicately aromatic, while also having depth and body to them. The late ripening season gives them a lightness that makes them extremely easy to drink, while also providing a complex depth of flavour.

Apart from flavour, the measurable qualities of the grapes are acid and sugar content. UK grapes normally have lower sugar levels and higher acidity than warmer regions. Sugar is sometimes added to produce around 11 percent alcohol in the fermented wine. The higher acidity allows the wine to age gracefully, giving freshness in youth, but mellowing with age. Some grape varieties will regularly harvest at higher acid levels than others and the winemakers have learnt to use the different varieties for different styles of wine, taking advantage of the acid. A medium-dry wine would taste flat and dull if lacking in acidity and high acid levels are *absolutely* required for the production of sparkling wines.

We all know that some years are blessed with sunny weather, while others are wetter and overcast. The variation in the weather is reflected by a variation in the vineyard harvest. The same factor explains why some vintages of Bordeaux are considered better than others. The whole picture is complex: the weather in any part of the season will only affect that stage of the vine's growth cycle. In 1997 we had some of the best late-summer weather of that decade, but the spring gave us a late frost; the result was that many vineyards produced very small crops, and were unable to take full advantage of the favourable year. In a cool climate the grower has to work around the challenges of the weather, minimising any risks and maximising the benefits.

Sparkling wine production is a common feature of many cool climate regions. These wines need acid to balance the fizz. In warmer regions the acid is added in the winery from a sack, but the classic balance can be achieved in the UK without any chemical adulteration. It is no surprise that Britain's growers have equipped themselves with the knowledge and skills to become masters at bottle fermenting their wines (producing sparkling wines by undergoing a second fermentation in the bottle). Many of these English sparkling wines have been heralded by the media as world class competitors.

When it comes to red wines, Britain is still an emerging talent. Most red grapes need superb sunshine to colour the grapes and acid levels in red wines need to be lower giving a softer style of wine. Recent new grape varieties such as Rondo and the availability of earlier-ripening clones of Pinot Noir have shown some possibilities. The resulting wines have a wide divergence of styles, from light burgundy-style to the fuller-bodied red wines based on Rondo. Oak barrels are often used to add another layer of flavour over the fruit. As winemaking skills develop, and more experience is gained, English and Welsh red wines will feature more often.

While the Southern Hemisphere is increasing its dominance on the wine market in the UK, people become accustomed to the heavy fruity wines, strong oak influence and their obvious flavours. Cool climates can make wines with the same clean purity, but (for me) they also can have more

interest, complex flavours, delicacy and natural refreshing acidity. These wines will always be "hand-crafted" because the high price of land and the cost of growing grapes in the UK discourages the mass production approach. The range of styles available can provide a match to almost any food or occassion. The pleasure of tasting different wines stems from knowing their origins. The grape variety, soils and climate play the deciding role in the wine's quality and every region has its own unique combination of these factors. However in a cool climate the variations are increased, and the effect of varietal flavours, soils and vineyard management practices play a far greater role. These wines get commented upon, create interest and give great pleasure.

ABOUT
WILL DAVENPORT

As well as being a chemistry graduate, Will Davenport has a wide experience of the wine industry. He has worked in Alsace, California and Australia, during which he studied for a degree in wine making at Roseworthy College (now part of Adelaide University). During two years working with a London wine merchant, he gained a Wine & Spirit Education Trust Diploma with Honours and developed a strong interest in international wine styles. He is a judge for the International Wine & Spirits Competition.

Since 1990 he has remained in the UK and has specialised in English wine making and viticulture. Making wine for Wellow Vineyards (Hants) over three vintages helped to develop his knowledge of English grape varieties and in 1991 he was convinced enough to plant his first vineyard at Horsmonden (Kent).

In 1993 Will moved to East Sussex, planting a vineyard specifically for sparkling wine production. 1995 saw the launch of the Horsmonden wine, which has gone on to win awards every year since. Will is considered one of the most experienced and professional people working in English wine today. He is almost unique, in that he relies on only organic methods in the vineyard and winery, believing that this is the way to maximise varietal and regional character in the wines.

English Wine Has Arrived

By Martyn Doubleday

With grape names like Muller-Thurgau, Reichensteiner, Schonburger, Bacchus, Huxelrebe and Kerner, you would be forgiven if you thought you were reading about German wines.

In the early days, those brave souls who had a bit of spare land and an ego for a vineyard next door, considered those German varieties the best for our northern climes. Unfortunately, they also considered that the German style was for us, too. Many of the pioneering wine makers also sought instruction from our German cousins. Hence, we began a style and a quality that was to give English wine a very bad name and become the focus of media jokes akin to estate agents and car dealers.

Poorly made wine, in un-sterile conditions, led to an abundance of wine faults. Have you ever had an egg sandwich just out of cling film? Well, that pong was on the bouquet of many a past offering. No wonder the jokes kept on coming!

Our bacon was saved with the arrival of New World wines, mainly from Australia and California. Affordable, good quality wine from Down Under became the nation's favourite. The second generation of English wine makers took notice. Those Aussies took a scientific approach and very soon knew the "ins and outs" of the grapes, fermentation methods and sterile bottling, not to mention marketing. English wine was soon to find a new way forward. Many wine makers went south to study and, indeed, some Aussie wine makers came over here and stayed.

STUNNING WINES

The fundamental rules for a good wine are: ripe berries with no rot, clean wine making and a vigilance during fermentation to avoid those egg sandwich aromas. This new approach was soon to produce some stunning wines.

To grow really ripe, clean grapes was not always possible in our climate, especially with Spring frosts to nip the tender primary shoots containing the best buds. At the other end of the season, the first frosts of winter often claimed the nearly ripe fruit, sending it to flab. A rainy summer, of course, brought disease. Oh, those mildews! However, new approaches to growing have taught our worthy band to read the signs of nature and monitor the days at the problem periods. Many are now expert in producing consistently good quality fruit essential to keep the flag flying.

In my opinion, wines in this tiny industry have not yet really found a style to call English and there are many different types to thrill our pallets. The original Germanic offering of acid-based wine made from unripe fruit and sweetened up with something called Sweet reserve, which is grape juice concentrate, covering a multitude of faults, has almost gone, thank goodness, and now tremendous advances have been made by passionate viticulturists and wine makers.

There are stunning **dry white** wines good enough to

Picture courtesy of New Wave Wines

rival some of the best of French, such as Muscadel and Sancerre. Fantastic, steely dry numbers with a fresh crispness and overtures of the English countryside - nettles, elder flower and other complex fruit flavours abound.

Some wine makers have used oak to help lift the fruit and here I must emphasize that the purpose has been not to make an oakey drink but just enough time in oak barriques to give a hint of toast or vanilla. This **fume** style is very much my favourite and Fortnum and Masons have chosen this as their own Label English Table Wine.

Another style that is becoming increasingly popular is the **off dry**, an ideal aperitif to go with canapés or starters. Modern wine-making techniques have enabled the vineyards to stop the fermentation process at just the right time when the grape sweetness and acid is in perfect balance and the old way of adding Sweet reserve is gone. It necessarily follows that we can also produce a stunning medium dry style for those who prefer it.

In exceptional years, by using late harvest grapes or berries infected with "noble rot" some enterprising vineyards have produced excellent dessert wines, perfectly balanced with a clean acidity to leave the mouth refreshed and without that feeling of woolly jumpers on one's teeth so often found in sweet wines from elsewhere; just think honeyed fruit flavours, ripe apricots, peaches and pineapples all rolled into one. These are real Ambrosia.

ROSE

Many experts think of Rose as a failed red or a sweetened up, poor quality white wine made a pretty pink to mug the first passer by. Well, maybe. But not here. I do think that is a style at which we in England and Wales can excel. Rose is not red wine mixed with white, as many so often think, but carefully selected fruit pressed with a little time on the red skins, just enough to extract the colour but not the tannins i.e. those bits that in young reds tend to leave a dryness on the teeth and tongue.

The Rose wine is bottled early, essential to capture its freshness. Young, fresh and fruity, summer meadows, picnics, barbecues and Oriental cuisine come to mind. Add to this vibrant pink hues, a perfect match to our modern lifestyles and the colourful cookery of today. Essential to enjoy on a perfect English summer day. NB. A Rose must be drunk when it is young. Find and orange coloured one and it is past its best.

FOUNDATION OF ENGLISHNESS

To sum up, English and welsh wines, in my opinion, have not developed into a generic style but reflect the very foundation of Englishness - individuality. The industry has many passionate personalities working away producing quality, world class wines which have for many years been successful in international competitions and up there with the best of them in many different categories.

I can say, hand on heart,that when tasting an English wine of whatever style mentioned above and knowing personally the hard work, the passion, the tears and the joys that it all entails to get a grape to the glass, the English wine industry deserves all the support we can give. Forget the old "sniggers." We can be proud that English wine has arrived.

ABOUT
MARTYN DOUBLEDAY

Martin Doubleday was a co-founder of Hidden Spring Vineyard at Horam, East Sussex. He planted the vineyard having left London to start a new career and pioneered rose production. His Sussex Sunset won 14 national and international awards. He also pioneered English red wine and his was the first to be sold at Fortnum and Masons. In 1989, he was among the first to use Aussie Winemaker.

Today he is a wine writer and broadcaster including for SKY News, LBC, London News Direct, Meridian News, Channel 4 News and radio 4. He also write for a number of newspapers and magazines including Brighton Argus, Limited Edition,

Careful Vine Selection Key To Developing Potential

By Carl Koenen,
New Wave Wines

Vines for red wine production in England currently account for over 11 per cent of the planted area with production levels at roughly 10 per cent. There are still those who remain sceptical about making red wines in England but these folk will not have been exposed to wines made from well grown and matured grapes following a quality conscious red wine making regime.

As the fruit ripens and the harvest season approaches minds turn to getting the winery ready for the long days and night shifts required to ensure that the grapes are processed while in optimum condition. As white grapes are by far the majority to 90 per cent then clearly most wineries will be set up for white wine making. Red wine making demands quite a different approach and this is were the dividing line is drawn between those growers who treat their red fruit as if it were white. These wines, whilst attractive and having a dedicated but limited following, will not capture the imagination of the claret, burgundy or sweaty saddle Australian Shiraz drinker.

Basically they will appear to be too light and lacking in

colour. Hence those that treat their red fruit as red fruit should be treated, will manage to attract the more critical connoisseur.

The red wine making campaign is all together different. The processing of the fruit can be long and labour intensive. The grape must has to stay in contact with the skins to extract colour and pumping over of the juice in the fermentation vessel is a vital part of colour and flavour extraction. Care must be taken to ensure that whilst you obtain colour you have not taken out too much of the rough and raw tannin that will unbalance the wine. Once the young wine has its colour, various rackings aside, the process of maturation begins. Malo-lactic fermentation will often play a role to gen'ly soften the acidity. When to bottle becomes an issue? Red wine should never be hurried and so patience really is a virtue.

Do wines that have undergone this type of regime pay dividends both for the producer and consumer alike? In our experience they certainly do.

The type of vines planted are a crucial factor. Their suitability to our climate and terrain remain key. We have found that the classic Bordeaux varieties do not perform here but Pinot Noir, the classic burgundian grape, shows great potential.

PINOT NOIR

Whilst the image of soupy deep, rich red burgundy tends to be the norm the reality is that Pinot Noir yields an elegant red wine with great finesse. Consider that in the USA this grape comes to the fore in the northern parts of California and further up the coast in Oregon and Washington State. In England this grape is used for base sparkling wines as well as red wines. Recent examples from the 1997, 1998 and 1999 vintage have shown a steady development in quality. The wines have admirers the world over and it is always a moment to savour when foreign wine makers and respected traditional English wine merchants gather like bees round a honey pot because somebody has told them that the English have made a red wine from Pinot Noir and it tastes like Pinot Noir.

Other important red grapes are Rondo and Dornfelder. These grapes produce wines with a full deep rich colour that is immediately appealing to traditional red wine lover.

New Wave Wines have three main red wines in their portfolio: Epoch I, Epoch Reserve and Pinot Noir. These wines are now offered under the Curious Grape label – formally Chapel Down. The Epoch I is a stylish and attractive red wine made from 60 percent Rondo and 40 percent Pinot Noir. It undergoes malo-lactic fermentation and aging in oak casks. The 2000 vintage is similar in many respects to fine red Loire wines such as Chinon or Bourgeuil.

BRING OUT THE BEST

The Epoch Reserve is 100 percent Rondo and is all-together a chunkier deeper red wine. The wine making follows the same form as that of the standard Epoch I but pure Rondo matures well and suggests southern Rhone, Rioja and north western Italy when you look for a comparison. There is an interesting spicy note to the wine with great fruit and sustaining tannins. Both the Epoch I and the Reserve will partner a whole range of classis roast meat dishes. Roast lamb and Epoch I are a super combination. With cheeses, and especially Stilton, these wines bring out the best in both cheese and wine alike.

Their Pinot Noir is a fascinating wine. Having used the initial pressings of this red fruit for base sparkling wine – early pressing extracts white juice – skin contact takes place on an increased ratio of skins to juice hence a fuller red appearance than might be expected. Following maturation for up to 12 months in a combination of different oak casks – mainly French wood as American oak tends to over-power the delicacy and fragrance of Pinot Noir – the resultant wine displays great Pinot Noir character and most importantly elegance and finesse.

Red vines are planted at all three of New Wave Wines vineyard sites: Tenterden, Lamberhurst in Kent and Carr Taylor at Westfield East Sussex. Recent additional plantings of Pinot Noir, Rondo and Dornfelder will come into full production at Tenterden from the 2002 harvest. Some of the Rondo from the Lamberhurst site is main in an attractive fruity un-oaked style with a strong bramble like aroma and flavour and sold mainly through the Lamberhurst vineyard shop.

New Wave Wines has an unrivalled range of wines and with the benefit of their three sites across Kent and Sussex and their state of the art winery at Tenterden offers visitors a superb insight into winemaking across the various disciplines of sparkling white and red.

English Sparkling Wine Now Winning Accolades Around The World

By Mike Roberts
RidgeView Wine Estate

The Australians and other new world wine makers take English sparkling wine very seriously. So seriously that they invited an English wine maker to speak at the Sparkling Wine Workshop in Melbourne.

The Cool Climate Wine Symposium is held every four years and gathered together eight of the world's foremost makers of sparkling wine under one roof. They came from such prominent names as Cloudy Bay, Domain Chandon, Pipers Brook, Brown Brothers, Hardy's and Iron Horse, several owned by the grand mark champagne houses. The ninth speaker was from RidgeView Estate in England.

Under the downs in Sussex you are looking at a geology almost identical to Champagne. The chalk downs continue under the channel forming the Paris basin and continuing up to the Marne Valley, the heart of Champagne. The weather too is similar, as you might expect bearing in mind how close we are. In terms of latitude this area is closer to Reims than to Luton! It is here in Sussex that both Nyetimber and RidgeView have established their vineyards that exclusively make sparkling wine from the Champagne grape varieties, Chardonnay, Pinot Noir and Meunier.

It was once said that Chardonnay could not be grown in England but that was with still wine in mind. Champagne is England's nearest appellation and both RidgeView and Nyetimber have tried to learn from their neighbours. Chardonnay, one of the cornerstones of Champagne, is also grown in Burgundy to make a fat luscious Meursault and Chablis but in Champagne they do not try to mimic that style. Instead, using the refreshing acidity and fruit flavours that come from this northerly climate, they make the quintessential sparkling wine. More vineyards in England are now planting the classic varieties and even as this article goes to press two new vineyards are being planted. To quote Joanna Simon in The Sunday Times: " ..Nyetimber and Ridgeview have proved that at least one small area of England can produce world class fizz."

In international competitions, English sparkling wines have won over twenty medals in just the last four years.

Recommended reading for sparkling wine lovers is Tom Stevenson's Champagne and Sparkling Wine Guide. Wines from around the world are reviewed. To quote Tom Stevenson, the author and world renowned expert on Champagne: "20 English wines are recommended by me in the 2002 edition, with six wines scoring 85 points or higher, which according to the book's definition is the sort of quality that Champagne has to be to warrant inclusion in my cellar. If a non-Champagne scores this high, it is of exceptional quality indeed!"

In fact 10 of the 20 wines in the guide scored more than 80 points, the score needed for a Champagne to be recommended. These wines came from five different vineyards including Nyetimber and RidgeView, along with Davenport, Bruisyard and Bearsted.

It really isn't surprising that the new world wine makers in Melbourne unanimously said: "We are so envious of your climate."

Tastes good - does you good

By Doreen Hillier - Bird, Windmill Vineyard

Wine definition:-

1. An alcoholic drink produced by the fermenting of grapes with water and sugar. 2. An alcoholic drink produced in this way from other fruits and flowers. *Source: Collins Concise Dictionary.*

The making of wine was man's very first leisure activity, the first activity that did not revolve around food gathering and the protection of territory.

It is thought that cave dwellers were the first to make an alcoholic drink using honey, which contains natural yeasts and sugar, and with the addition of water ferments quite readily.

MEAD

Mead, or honey wine, has been made throughout history and has been used in religious ceremonies all over the world. Mead has been held to have magical properties, probably because turning honey and water into a delectable drink which had the added appeal of making life seem much less hard must have seemed magical to someone ignorant of the process of fermentation.

The ancient Greeks had orgies which went on for a whole month in celebration of their various gods, at which was consumed large quantities of Mead. Both the Saxons and the Norse people drank Mead at all wed-

Doreen and Tom Hillier-Bird

ding feasts which also lasted for a whole month and is the origin of our modern word 'honeymoon.'

Honey is the product of a bee hive and is made by the bees collecting nectar and pollen from flowers. The pollen is made into a substance called beeswax, which the bee transforms into honeycomb, a special storage space for the nectar which the bee regurgitates in the form of honey. While the bee has the nectar in its stomach it adds an enzyme which preserves the honey and actually produces a perfectly natural antibiotic which, of course, is why grandma always gave you honey for a sore throat and why it always worked. The recipe changes according to the flower nectar and the season and therefore the human metabolism never becomes immune to it. Not that granny knew all this; she just knew that honey was good for you.

Honey stored in beeswax contains some of the pollen grains

that the bee collected to make the beeswax and hay fever sufferers will very often get relief if they eat honey made from whatever the plant is that causes the allergy. As with all "natural" remedies it is a long-term treatment. A spoonful of honey a day keeps the allergy away.

Alcoholic drinks containing honey have been made for many centuries. The mixing of honey with other fruits such as black grapes (Pyement) produced stronger alcohol levels in the days before sugar had been discovered, both cane and beet varieties, than by using just the natural fructose of the fruit. Apple juice and honey (Cyser) produces a drink reminiscent of sherry.

Between the 13th and 18th Century, a blend of honey and malted barley produced a brew known as 'Braggot.' This had various seasonal fruits added to it to "improve the flavour" and was the base for 'wassail,' a Saxon drink produced in particular for Christmas Eve and Twelfth Night. Herbs were added to this mainly to make the drinker drunker quicker! Both Rosemary and Bog Myrtle are said to enhance the effects of alcohol.

ELDERBERRY

All hedgerow fruits have been used at some time to make into wine. Elderberries, being so numerous in the hedgerows, have always been made into a very full bodied red wine, full of tannin and therefore said to be good for the heart and the blood. A vintage Elderberry wine, aged for at least two years, was called by the old countrymen 'Elder Port' which has a strong mellow taste, very like an expensive port wine. Today's scientists have of course declared red wine good for the heart so the old countrymen were not so far from the mark after all.

Elderflowers, on the other hand, produce a white wine with a delicate bouquet. Should you need an excuse, Elderflower relieves stress, is relaxing and a light sedative, a wonderful wine for a hot summer's day, to sit in the shade of your favourite tree and drink. Elderflower Spritzer made from Elderflower wine and a sparkling spring water is the epitome of a "perfect day."

SILVER BIRCH

Silver Birch wine is made from the sap of the Silver Birch, collected in very early Spring by tapping the trunk of the tree, rather as rubber trees are tapped and drawing off the sap into a container. The sap is then fermented to a dry white wine rather reminiscent of a 'Martini.' This is the basis of the Russian drink 'Kvass. which is made from birch sap, mint and yeast. The main active constituent of the sap is methyl salicylate which is similar to aspirin and is an anti-inflammatory analgesic. Birch wine has there-fore been used for the treatment of rheumatism and arthritis for centuries. In the Scandinavian countries it has another unusual use - to stop hair loss in males - although whether one rubs it on or drinks it I am unsure!

DANDELION

The first warm suns of Spring bring out the gardener's en-emy. Dandelions, the bright flowers of which make a quite unusual if slightly bitter white wine. Actually, Dandelions are a very useful plant - wine from the flowers, coffee from the root and salad from the leaves. Dandelion wine is useful in supplying trace elements to the system, it is diuretic and combats uric acid accumulation in the tissues.

ROSE

Rather more emotive is rose petal wine. Usually highly scented roses produce a wonderful bouquet to a light dry wine, the colour of which depends on the colour of the rose, red roses producing a rose and yel-low roses producing a white wine. Rose petal wine is supposed to be sopo-rific and relaxing - another summer afternoon drink.

All through the ages man has made alcoholic drinks from all the plants surrounding him and used the medicinal properties of these plants to improve his health and well being.

In modern ages grapes have become the fruit that wine is made from. When the Roman legions marched across what is now Europe they planted their Mediterranean grapes everywhere because they were not keen on the local brews made from other fruits and gradually the other wines have almost been forgotten.

When the Romans came to Britain they planted their vineyards with each villa having a vineyard and winery. When the Romans left, Britain was already a Christian country and the monasteries took over vine growing to provide wine for religious ceremonies.

Over the intervening centuries, the fashion has changed to the drinking of wines made from a selection of grape cultivars grown for their flavours and juice containing properties.

Fruit or 'Country Wines' are now produced by just a few vintners and a sprinkling of amateurs who between them keep old recipes alive.

Be brave. Try some of the 'Country Wines.' After all they taste good as well as do you good and they are very versatile in their use. One you have tasted a raspberry pavlova using raspberry wine in the filling, Pavlova will never be the same again. Or Gooseberry Fool with just a touch of sweet gooseberry wine.

Bon Appetite.

Glossary Of UK Popular Grapes

WHITE

Siegerrebe
Commonly harvested in mid-September. Not a very big cropper but very good quality - high sugars, low acids and a very aromatic, spicy flavour.

Madeline Angevine
A reliable cropper if the right "clone" is selected. Full and fruity character, with good sugar levels and lowish acids. Produces a very distinctive wine with a good fruit bouquet.

Huxelrebe
A very good cropper with good sugar levels but sometimes a little higher in acidity. Commonly used in wines of sweeter styles. It has a very rich, distinctive character and develops well in bottle with a bit of age.

Reichensteiner
Tends to be "over vigorous" in the vineyard and needs a lot of control but the wine is rich and adds an important dimension to blends.

Bacchus
A very distinctive aromatic variety. Full of English hedgerows, elderflower and nettles. Low yields produce intensive flavour - a very special wine.

Phoenix And Orion

Hybrids of interspecific crosses. they have the advantage of good yields, very clean grapes and sound wines. Phoenix, a cross between Seyval Blanc and Bacchus is the more promising of the two.

Muller Thurgau

The most famous of North European varieties, now superceded by more modern varieties. Moderate cropper but wines tend to be of good quality - flowery, spicy and well balanced. Tends to be used in blends.

Seyval Blanc

The original "hybrid," producing very good yields of extremely "clean" grapes. The wine produced tends to be less fruity than many but blends well and is well suited to oak fermentation and sparkling wine production.

Schonberger

Regular but low yielder. A cross of Pinot Noir and Muscat. When fully ripe it has a pink tinge and a muscaty flavour. Aromatic, spicy and well suited to an off dry single variety wine in most years. Also enhances a blend.

Chardonnay

A late harvester which is seldom successful as a still wine but which is being used increasingly in making high quality sparkling wine.

Pinot Blanc

Not widely distributed. This newish variety requires a good site and careful management. It is being used to make interesting varietal wines as well as a base for sparkling wines.

Pinot Gris
A variety with lower acidity which is generally used in the production of sparkling wines.

Auxerrois
One of the earliest varieties planted in the UK. A good, steady, middle-of-the road workhorse with good yields and lower acid levels.

Faberrebe
High in natural sugar and with a fruity, crisp acidity, it is a good partner for other varieties, especially Muller Thurgau.

Ortega
Produces a rich and zesty wine with good balance. Goes well with oak and can also produce "Noble Rot" if sugar levels are high enough.

Regner
Ripens early with high sugar and low acid levels. Not easy to find in the UK.

REDS

Triomphe
An early hybrid variety. Very good fruit character and reasonable colour.

Rondo
A new variety, approved by Brussels. It is very deep in colour and has a very heavy wine character (good tannins).

Dornfelder

Lighter in colour but good sized fruit and fairly "clean" grapes. The wine tends to be light and fruity although when fully ripe this need not be so.

Pinot Noir

Tends to be one of the last varieties picked. A red grape with a while juice Pinot Noir is a classic variety of the Champagne region of France. Used to make red wine, rose and sparkling wine.

Dunkelfelder

A variety which produces massive colour but generally only a small crop. Is best blended with other red varieties.

Leon Millot

One of the first red varieties to be grown commercially., it has now been largely overtaken by other varieties.

49

WHO WE ARE

The English Wine Producers (EWP) is the marketing arm for the UK wine industry. Its work and role in marketing and promoting English wines and vineyards complements the legislative and official work the UKVA undertakes for English wines.

Originally formed by a few of England's leading independent producers for the purpose of promoting their wines to the trade, media and consumer, EWP now retains a sizeable membership of different vineyards, who all share the same enthusiasm to promote English wines to a wide audience. EWP's members represent over three-quarters of England's total wine production, so are a major force within the its wine industry. EWP is now also supported by the UKVA, which enables more generic work to be developed. UKVA and EWP work closely together, and consequently, any member of EWP also has to be a UKVA subscriber.

The forming of an association to promote English wines came at a time of increasing interest in what England was producing, as new winemakers, winning styles and commercial quantities were introduced to and noticed by the wine trade and wine writers, and in turn wine drinkers. EWP members exhibit their wines under one banner, enabling buyers to taste an extensive selection of wines, and showing that England too can compete on quality, price and availability.

WHAT WE DO

There are four main areas of EWP's work.

1) Information access: EWP is the useful central access to information on all aspects of English wines, from putting you in touch with vineyards or sending out of contact details or brochures to specific information on vineyards, information on where to find the wines, wine production and so forth.

2) Events: once a year EWP organises a trade tasting to which wine writers and trade buyers are invited to taste the largest range of latest wines from its members. This ensures more coverage of English wines, and puts writers and buyers in direct contact with vineyards. EWP works with UKVA on their annual competition and other events aimed at the industry, but which attracts interest from the wine press. It is important to keep the wine press informed; they write up about English wines and it is you, the wine drinker, who reads about them and buys the wines!

There are a number of English wine-related events and activities for the wine consumer that take place throughout the year that involve EWP, and these are described more fully elsewhere in this book.

3) Website: englishwineproducers.com was set up in 2000 as the industry's official website. It is a source of up to date information on vineyards, wines, English wine events and many other aspects of English wines generally. This also includes a monthly updated newsletter and tips on what to do if you grow vines yourself and a helpline for any queries.

4) Keeping the wine press and other important groups updated with news and information on English wine and vineyards, with press releases and regular dialogue. We also supply information and wines to wine educators to assist with obtaining a good selection of English wines when talking to wine groups around the country.

Importantly, English Wine Producers is there to help with any information you require about any aspects of English wine; we can be contacted by phone, fax, e-mail or through the website!

EVENTS ON THE ENGLISH WINE

CALENDAR

ENGLISH WINE WEEK

English Wine Week is a national campaign to focus on English vineyards and wines, and their ideal marriage with regional food. The campaign takes place over the week of the Whitsun Bank Holiday which is usually summer half term holiday in many schools.

During English Wine Week, many vineyards are open to the public, organising special events and activities, as well as offering tours and tastings. A number of vineyards not normally open to the public also participate. Many also link up with outlets within the on and off trade. English Wine Week is promoted widely through the press (national and regional), tourist information centres, and participating outlets. Listings of events and activities taking place are also to be found on the EWP website (www.englishwineproducers.com).

About 95 vineyards throughout central, eastern and southern England are open to the public. In many cases full visitors' facilities are offered, from guided tours and tastings, restaurants/cafe/tea rooms to shops and other attractions for all the family. Many of these vineyards are found in some of the prettiest and most visited parts of the country. You can enjoy the hospitality at an English vineyard when you are visiting another part of the country, and see at first hand how wines are produced, and taste before you buy, without having to cross the Channel!

For information contact English Wine Producers.

UKVA ENGLISH & WELSH WINE OF THE YEAR COMPETITION

There has been a national competition since 1974. Organised by the governing body of the industry, the UK Vineyards Association, the competition is now known as the English & Welsh Wine of the Year Competition.

The wines are entered in to sections, depending upon the volume of wine in bottle available for sale on the day of the presentation of awards:

The competition takes place in June, and each year is hosted by a different UK wine-producing region. The results are issued on the day of the competition, when competitors are contacted, and a press release sent out to the wine press. The awards are officially announced at the awards presentation ceremony at the House of Lords in July.

The judges who make up the tasting panel are selected by the panel's Chairman, and over the years have included tasters from many walks of the wine trade, from journalists to wine buyers, wine writers, wine merchants and wine makers. The wines are tasted blind and marked to international standards. The judging panel each year includes members of the wine trade or press local to the region in which the event is taking place.

Medal winners can display their awards as a sticker on their winning wines, which highlights their success to you the consumer.

ENGLISH WINE FESTIVAL

The English Wine Festival takes place each year in September and is a recognized show case for the products of UK vineyards. Thousands of consumers flock to the festival every year to take advantage of the unique opportunity to taste(and buy) selections of wines from throughout the vine growing districts of the UK.

Annual English Wine and Regional Food Festival

The annual English Wine and Regional Food Festival was established in 1975 by Christopher Ann, The English Wine Centre, Alfriston in East Sussex. The Festival aimed to act as a show-case for English wine, ideally situated in the South East of England in an area long renowned for its fine fruit. The counties of Kent, East and West Sussex and Surrey have about half the national acreage of vineyards. Whilst primarily an event for the South East, the Wine Festival has always attracted vineyards from further afield and visitors from all over the county.

Since 1975, The Wine Festival has enjoyed great success at a number of venues in East Sussex, maintaining its status as the UK's longest running Wine Festival.

The Wine Festival has now found a new home at Bentley Wildfowl and Motor Museum, Halland near Lewes, East Sussex. Bentley is a popular East Sussex County Council owned tourist attraction, with over 100 acres encompassing beautiful parkland, walled garden, woodland and renowned wildfowl reserve. It also houses an unusual veteran, vintage and classic car collection, and together with a miniature steam railway and children's play area, offers a wide mix of attractions to underpin the event.

The UK's longest running Wine Festival

54

The Wine Festival very much complements Bentley's programme of annual events including a midsummer Food and Drink Show and a nationally recognised autumn WoodFair. The full programme and details of the Wine Festival are available on the website www.eastsussexcc.gov.uk/env/events.

The Wine Festival takes place each year on the first weekend of September. The dates for 2002 are Saturday 7 and Sunday 8 September, and the Festival will retain the traditional features incorporating the main marquee of wine and regional food producers, wine competition, wine tasting stage, grape treading, barbecue and jazz entertainment. In association with a Taste of the South East, the Festival will also include tutored cheese tastings, alongside the popular wine tasting stage. The Festival organisers will also be seeking out vineyards from other areas of the country, and additional food products which specifically complement wine.

Entry to the 28th English Wine Festival, including all the attractions of Bentley: Adults £10 or £8 in advance which includes wine and food tastings, souvenir glass and programme; Children £3.50.

Do You Know?

The English wine industry has developed since the first re-plantings after the Second World War - the 1952 plantings by Sir Guy Salisbury Jones and about 10 acres of vines in the early 1960s.

Today there are over 2,000 acres, 400 vineyards and 50 wineries producing three million bottles of wine a year.

The vines are European Vitis Vinifera varieties.

English wine is exported to France, Germany, Belgium, Japan, Australia and other major wine growing countries around the world.

It is regularly served in the House of Commons, House of Lords and the Glyndebourne Opera House.

English wine regularly beats its European counterparts in blind tastings in the UK and abroad. Recently producers received over 50 awards at the International Wine Challenge, one of the top competitions.

Barnsole Vineyard

Situated in Kent, Barnsole Vineyard produces a range of white wines, which have achieved Quality Wine status. A red wine will be available in 2003

Barnsole Vineyard is open every day from April to October and, depending on the weather, most days during winter.

Visitors are welcome and there are free mini-tours and wine tastings as well as full guided tours for which a small fee is charged.

The vineyard has its own winery so in addition to looking at the vines it is possible to see the full wine-making process.

Main grape varieties are Reichensteiner, Huxelrebe and Schonburger with Rondo and Regent to produce red wine.

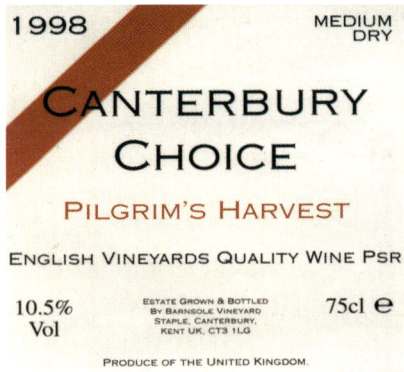

1998   MEDIUM DRY

CANTERBURY CHOICE

PILGRIM'S HARVEST

ENGLISH VINEYARDS QUALITY WINE PSR

10.5% Vol   ESTATE GROWN & BOTTLED BY BARNSOLE VINEYARD STAPLE, CANTERBURY, KENT UK, CT3 1LG   75cl ℮

PRODUCE OF THE UNITED KINGDOM.

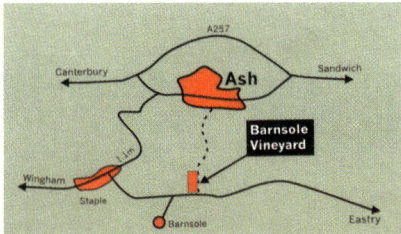

CANTERBURY CHOICE
Quality Wine from
Barnsole Vineyard
Fleming Road,
Staple, Canterbury,
Kent CT3 1LG
Tel: 01304 812530
MOB: 07770 482883
Website: www.barnsole.co.uk

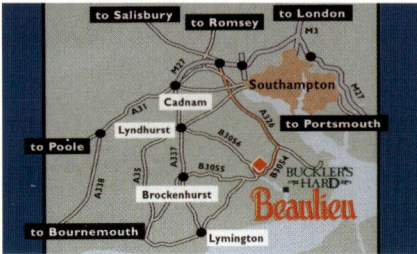

**National Motor Museum
Beaulieu,
Brockenhurst,
Hampshire.
Tel: 01590 612345**

The wines of Beaulieu Vineyard are an enjoyable additional treat for those visiting the estate - more famous for its National Motor Museum than for vine growing

In fact, grape growing and wine making at Beaulieu go back as far as the 13th Century, when monks at Beaulieu Abbey planted a vineyard to obtain the wines they needed for their ceremonies.

In the 1950s, Lieut., Col., Gore-Brown and his wife Margaret took up residence near the Beaulieu Estate and soon became post-war pioneers of UK viticulture by resuscitating vine growing at Beaulieu.

Beaulieu Abbey wine became famous during the 1960s and its makers were also renowned for their support of viticulture in several parts of England and Wales.

The link between the Gore-Brown's vineyard and the Beaulieu Estate is that Ralph Montagu was Mrs. Gore-Brown's godson and she and her husband willed the vineyard to him upon their death.

Today, dry white wines made from Huxelrebe, Muller-Thurgau, Reichensteiner and Seyval Blanc are made at Valley Vineyards and sold at the National Motor Museum shop. Recently Bacchus has been added to the vineyard.

Crisp, dry white wines are a pleasantly surprising bonus for visitors to the Museum. Beaulieu is also famous for its "Beaulieu Bubbly."

Beaulieu and the Montagu family have played a leading role in UK viticulture since the 1960s, participating in vineyard associations and hosting the English Wine Festival and other wine-related events.

The winner of the UK's top annual wine award receives it every year on the terrace of the House of Lords - courtesy of Lord Montagu.

BEAULIEU
ENGLISH TABLE WINE

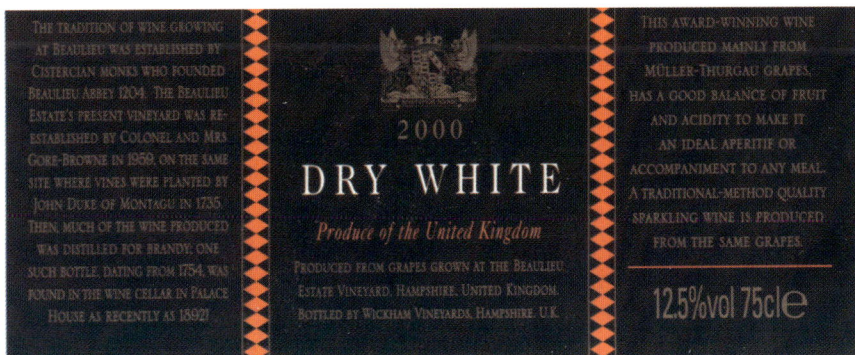

THE TRADITION OF WINE GROWING AT BEAULIEU WAS ESTABLISHED BY CISTERCIAN MONKS WHO FOUNDED BEAULIEU ABBEY 1204. THE BEAULIEU ESTATE'S PRESENT VINEYARD WAS RE-ESTABLISHED BY COLONEL AND MRS GORE-BROWNE IN 1959, ON THE SAME SITE WHERE VINES WERE PLANTED BY JOHN DUKE OF MONTAGU IN 1735. THEN, MUCH OF THE WINE PRODUCED WAS DISTILLED FOR BRANDY. ONE SUCH BOTTLE, DATING FROM 1754, WAS FOUND IN THE WINE CELLAR IN PALACE HOUSE AS RECENTLY AS 1892!

2000

DRY WHITE

Produce of the United Kingdom

PRODUCED FROM GRAPES GROWN AT THE BEAULIEU ESTATE VINEYARD, HAMPSHIRE, UNITED KINGDOM. BOTTLED BY WICKHAM VINEYARDS, HAMPSHIRE. U.K.

THIS AWARD-WINNING WINE PRODUCED MAINLY FROM MÜLLER-THURGAU GRAPES. HAS A GOOD BALANCE OF FRUIT AND ACIDITY TO MAKE IT AN IDEAL APERITIF OR ACCOMPANIMENT TO ANY MEAL. A TRADITIONAL-METHOD QUALITY SPARKLING WINE IS PRODUCED FROM THE SAME GRAPES.

12.5%vol 75cl℮

Carter's Vineyard

**Green Lane,
Boxted
Colchester,
Essex C04 5TS
Tel: 01206 271136
Fax: 01206 273625
www.cartersvineyards.co.uk**

"Success Breeds Success"

People who come to know about vineyards also quickly come to realize that many own ers are anything but farmers, often including professionals ranging through lawyers, doctors, dentists, IT specialists and, in Mary Mudd's case, optometry.

When she first bought her 40 acre site it was no more than two large corn fields with a dip in the middle and a small stream. Today she and her husband have turned it into a woodland landscape of lakes, wild flower meadows and a seven acre vineyard.

"Growing grapes is an absolute delight for they are endlessly interesting. Our early vines established well in the gravely soil and the first fruit, when it came, was wonderful. I was as proud of my first wines as one would be of a child."

In 12 years Mary has learned a great deal about vines and wines and has studied for various wine certificates and diplomas. She learnt wine making at Plumpton Agricultural College near Lewes in Sussex.

Learning about one's palate andt one's ability to discrimi-

nate the many aspects of wine such as grape variety, ageing and wine making techniques makes the prospect of tasting any wine exciting. Producing the best possible wine from the fruit you grow is also a fascinating craft.

Today, visitors come here to see the vineyard and buy the wines also find the alternative energy project and the conservation areas an added interest. They can enjoy walking through the several different habitats that have been crerated to encourage a range of bird birds and other wildlife, the ancient hedgerows and the wailfflower meadows all of which contrast admirably with the neat, regimented rows of vines.

The vineyard is not connected to mains electricity or water and two wind turbines and solar panels charge a large battery which runs the business. "People always find it interesting that while we have no mains power we have computers, a web site and credit card facilities without mains power."

The vineyard is close to Colchester, England's oldest town and Carter's Vineyards' wine labels feature the town's long and colourful history with names such as King Coel, St Helena and Boadicea.

Most of the wine is sold to visitors but specialty shops in the area and Colchester businesses and local government offices are major customers. Many visitors come in prebooked groups for a wine tasting evening and supper. A small fee enables visitors to take a tour of the vineyard and winery, see a video presentation taste five or so wines.

Mary is invited each year to take her wines to germany to sell at the Wine festival held in Colchester's twin town of Wetzlar. The French partner is Avignon and the wine is exhibited at their annual Fair and enjoyed at several restaurants there.

Carter's Vineyards produce white, red, rose and sparkling wines not only from their own grapes but also from those of around ten other vineyards. Carter's wines have now won many competitions and as Mary says: "word gets around and success breeds success."

"In the UK, we should be proud of the fact that we can produce crisp, dry, fruity white wines and excellent sparkling wines.

"I find there is a willingness locally to support an English wine grower and customers come back again and again. They like to serve the wine to visitors and present it as gifts and, if they travel to Europe they will take some bottles of Colchester wine for their hosts.

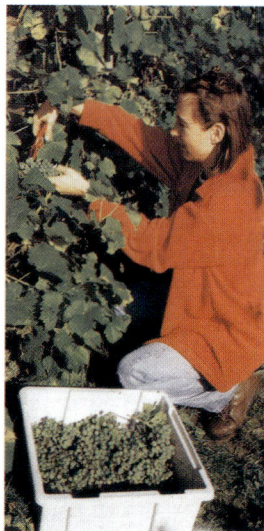

Chevelswarde Vineyard

Chevelswarde Vineyard is located in the extreme south of Leicestershire and produces dry and medium dry white wines. Production of the grapes is entirely organic and controlled by the Soil Association under Certification Symbol No. DO3M since 1975. The vineyard/farm shop is open daily between 9 am and 6 pm. Visitors to the vineyard are requested to phone or e-mail in advance of their visit to ensure that someone is available to show them round.

**The Belt,
South Kilworth,
Near Lutterworth,
Leicestershire LE17 6DX
Email:
john@chevel.freeserve.co.uk
Website:
www.chevelswardeorganics.co.uk**

Chevelswarde Vineyard is to be found at the end of a "bumpy lane" sloping down to a tributary of the River Avon of Shakespeare fame. Its award winning wines can be tasted and bought from the farm shop, open daily. The shop also has a wide range of organic fruit and vegetables for sale. Organically grown ciders and juices are also available.

The vineyard is located in Leicestershire although only a golf course and a field from the river which is the boundary with Northamptonshire.

It was planted during the late Spring of 1973, making it the oldest organic vineyard in Britain.

Owners, John and Ruth Daltry, began to grow vines organically after the use of fertilizers produced such lush growth that the wood did not ripen properly and nearly all the season's new wood died over winter. They joined the Soil Association and used organic techniques from then on, receiving Soil Association Organic Certification in 1975. A big advantage of using organic methods is that it is friendly to wildlife, evidenced by the high population of birds on the property. Also, there is minimal pollution of water which inevitably seeps through the ground from winter rains. The water supply companies spend vast sums on water purification to remove pesticides and fertilisers from water to make it safe to drink.

The vineyard is in a relatively sheltered position. The shelter has been enhanced by planting a number of mostly native trees around the perimeter.

The site is broadly south east facing which is near ideal as it catches the morning sunshine. This is best because as the day warms up clouds tend to build so afternoons are not as sunny as mornings.

In the beginning, John and Ruth sought advice from wine growers about which vines to plant and the result was that Mueller-Thurgau were chosen, the most popular variety at that time. Unfortunately, it is rather disease prone and not a very reliable cropper. Since those early days, better varieties have been developed and this Winter some of the Meuller-Thurgau vines have been grubbed to make room for three rows of Phoenix which is quite highly disease resistant and, most importantly, produces a very drinkable wine.

Chevelswarde has been awarded 'Commended' three times at the Mercian Vineyards Association Annual Tasting which is carried out in line with international standards.

Chilford Hall Vineyard

**Chilford Hall Vineyard,
Balsham Road,
Linton,
Cambridgeshire,
CB1 6LE
Tel: 01223 895600
Fax: 01223 895605
Web-site at
HYPERLINK
http:www.chilfordhall.co.uk**

C hilford Hall Vineyard at Linton near Cambridge is bringing some of its older wines to the fore for special tastings by visitors during Wine Week, held every year during the first week of June.

The Vineyard adds older wines, from the 70's, 80's or early 90's, to the tastings that accompany the vineyard's guided winery tour. While Chilford Hall has occasionally shown older wines at trade events, they are rarely shown to the public at large.

Simon Alper, Chilford Hall's Managing Director says, "Our English Wines have always aged remarkably well, confounding many tasters with their honeyed aromas and dry flavours. I have astonished respected French producers by serving our older wines with Roquefort cheese and I am delighted to be able to use Wine Week to show another side to the quality of our wines."

Chilford Hall gained recognition for its current and old wines in the 2001 East Anglian Wine of the Year Competition with a total of one Gold Award, 4 Bronze Awards and 2 Commendations.

Simon Alper adds, "We are delighted at the recognition we received for our wines, particularly the old ones. We do try to impress on people that white wines do not need to be drunk up quickly; in fact they will often become fuller and more interesting and flavourful over a period of three to eight years".

Chilford Hall Vineyard was established in 1972, producing its first crop in 1974. It has been making quality wines that have won wide recognition and many awards since. The knowledge and experience gained from over 25 years of wine making has helped to produce a fine range of wines, some suitable for drinking with food, others more suited to drink on their own. As well as enjoying growing popularity in the UK, Chilford Hundred wines are exported to Holland, France and California.

Visit Chilford Hall and see how wine is made, stroll around our vineyard trail and taste our new wines. Tour Price : Adults £4.50: Groups at £3.75, Children free. Evening tours are also available by prior arrangement. The Vineleaf Cafe is open for light meals and refreshments and the vineyard shop which sells our wines, gifts and specialty foods.

Simon Alper

Chiltern Valley Wines

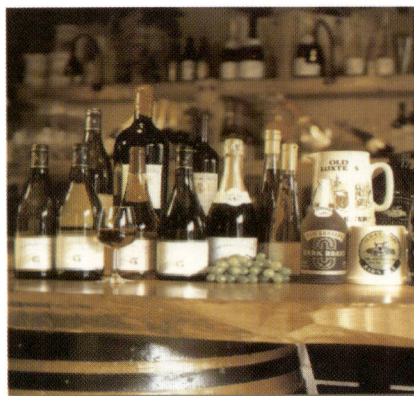

**Old Luxters Vineyard,
Winery & Brewery,
Hambleden,
Henley-On-Thames,
Oxfordshire RG9 6JW.
Tel: 01491 638330.
Fax: 01491 638645**

When turning off the Henley to Marlow Road (A4155 at the Hambleden turning) no one would be surprised if you were to be impressed at the magnificent countryside as you made your way up the valley deep into the Chiltern Hills. This area, swirling with rare red kites, beautiful rolling hills and unspoiled villages with welcoming Pubs, nestling in the valleys, has long since been designated an area of outstanding natural beauty. You would be foregiven, however, for your surprise at discovering one of Britain's best kept secrets, similarly set in the heart of the beautiful Hambleden Valley, Old Luxters Vineyard, Winery & Brewery, the home of Chiltern Valley Wines.

Since the early 1980s, when Old Luxters planted their first vineyard and created one of the most modern wineries in Europe, at that time, housed in the ancient farm barn and associated buildings, the reputation of Chiltern Valley Wines gained meteoric acclaim. In the first decade or so they won almost every national wine award available and very many international one's too, exceeding seventy. No wonder their wines have exported to over a dozen countries and are consumed in palaces and on picnics, in top restaurants, banks, boardrooms and by the confident yet discerning anywhere. Don't take my word for it. Just follow the signs to the winery and further surprises will await you after you pass the vineyard and turn into what was the old farmyard. There you will find the winery and cellar shop, open each day, including weekends and offering free tasting of each of their great range of wines.

Chiltern Valley offer a choice of eight dry, including two fabulous "champagnes." one pink and one white. The Vineyard also makes red wine, rose and a delicious medium dry, medium 'Special Cuvee' and, of course, their famous "Luxters dessert," recently acclaimed by Gilly Goolden. Perhaps what makes the cellars so unique is that since 1990 when Old Luxters Farm Brewery was set up, alongside the winery and state-of-the-art bottling facilities, you can also taste a huge range of traditional cask and bottle conditioned real ales direct from the brewery and at the new 'Gordon Brown,' halved rates of excise duty.

Still more, for it is here at Old Luxters that more recently they have turned their hand to the production of a range of very fine liqueurs, including 'Sloe Gin,' 'Damson Gin,' and 'Apricot Brandy' and 'Cherry Brandy.' Don't leave without tasting the 'Wild Strawberry Liqueur' which I found just fabulous, espe-

cially when added to their fizz, though don't tell them where you got the idea. They also make a plum based liqueur which tasted to me like a fine Port.

No wonder again that Old Luxters Wines, ales and their liqueurs were selected by the Royal Household to grace the shelves of the Royal Farm Shop at Windsor. Their awards speak for their wines but the wines speak for themselves. Tasting is believing.

Danebury Vineyards

Situated in Hampshire, Danebury Vineyards produces white and sparkling wines characterised by
their clean, crisp and fruity flavour.

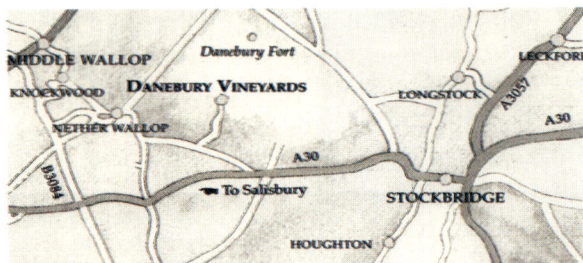

Danebury Cossack is a refreshingly dry
sparkling wine made from a blend of the
Auxerrois and Rulander grape varieties, planted
in 1988. The grapes are picked, with extreme care, by hand, using only
fruit in its prime. After malolactic fermentation the wine is bottled,
where it then goes through a second fermentation, producing the distinctive taste of a high quality sparkling wine.

Danebury Pyrrhus is a crisp, fruity wine made from the
Schonburger grape, also planted in 1988. Again the grapes are picked
by hand and the juice is put through a cold fermentation process, which
accentuates the fresh, fruity character of this quality white wine. Both
these wines are named after Danebury trained Epsom Derby winners
of the 1840's.

The vineyards cover an area of seven acres and are on gen-
tly sloping south facing fields, surrounded by a windbreak of beech
trees. The chalk and flint stone in the region means that the grapes
develop a balanced level of acidity and the long summer days allow

for maximum ripening. In 1996, two further varieties of grape were planted, Bacchus and Madaleine Angevine and 2001 saw the first significant harvest from them.

Visitors to the vineyard are very welcome between 9 am and 4 pm by appointment only. In addition to wine tasting, visitors can arrange to enjoy specially prepared meals that are designed to accompany the wines.

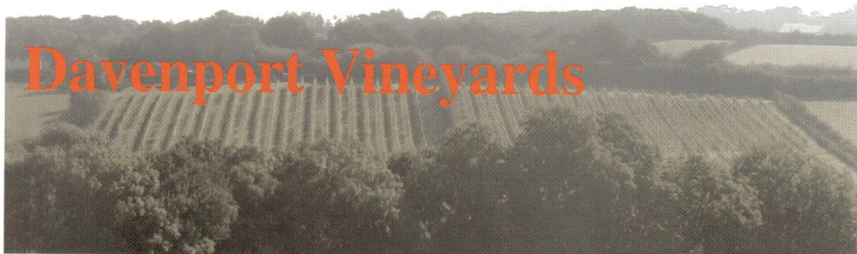

Davenport Vineyards

Limney Farm,
Castle Hill,
Rotherfield TN6 3RR,
East Sussex.
Tel: 01892-852380
Fax: 01892-852781
Email: info@davenportvineyards.co.uk
Web site: www.davenportvineyards.co.uk

D avenport wines have frequently featured among the award winners at national and international wine competitions, winning over forty awards in the last six years. During 2001 Davenport wines were awarded three medals at the UK Vineyards Association Wine of the Year competition and one award at the Wine Magazine International Wine Challenge. The Horsmonden dry white has featured twice among the top three wines in the CLA wine of the year competition since 1997.

Davenport Vineyards started with the planting of a small plot of vines at Horsmonden, Kent in 1991. The land is part of a commercial apple farm. Will Davenport was then working full time for a winery in Hampshire and caring for the vines on weekends and holidays. In 1992 the search started for a suitable site to develop into a commercial wine production unit.

Their second site, Limney Farm was found to be ideal because it is geographically close to the existing vineyard at Horsmonden, it is extremely good land for planting further vines and there was a good range of dairy buildings for use as a winery.

The first grapes were pressed in October 1993, and the wine was available for sale from 1995. Since then grapes have been pressed every autumn and all the wine has been sold within two years of harvest.

Most of the wine is sold through small independent outlets (restaurants, hotels, wine shops, etc.) and some has been sold outside the South-East to trade and private customers.

Davenport Vineyards was chosen as the English wine supplier to the Millennium Dome throughout 2000 and is currently supplying about 50 retail businesses with their wine. Wines are also sold to private customers by the case and Davenport Vineyards has a web site with facilities for ordering wine on-line. Davenport wines are delivered to addresses throughout the UK.

In 1997 Davenport Vineyards decided to develop a new sparkling wine as part of their range. English sparkling wine has received much media attention recently and is considered by some to be the future of English wine. The first 1997 vintage was awarded a Bronze medal at the UK Vineyards Association Wine of the Year competition, and the 1998 won a Silver medal last year. The decision has been a very positive step for Davenport Vineyards and the

wines have sold well. Excellent reviews have been received in Tom Stevenson's annual Champagne & Sparkling Wine Guide.

The involvement in sparkling winemaking has caused Davenport Vineyards to come under pressure for space in the winery, as sparkling wine needs to be stored for two to three years before sale. A new bottle storage building is under preparation. As the new store will be purpose built, the quality of the sparkling wines should benefit from temperature controlled storage (the current building used for storing bottled wine is a traditional agricultural building with no insulation, originally designed as a hay store).

As a result of successful wine making and a strong demand for his wines, Will Davenport has generated substantial business as a consultant to other vineyards. He currently advises about fifteen other vineyards (from small hobbies to medium-sized commercial businesess) on grape growing and winemaking matters. Some of these vineyards do not have winemaking facilities and so use the winery facilities at Limney Farm (which is considered to be one of the best equipped wineries in the country) to process their fruit. Many of these vineyards also have taken the opportunity to produce quality sparkling wines,a process which can only be done with expensive equipment and experienced winemaking. Davenport Vineyards has the facilities to complete the sparkling wine process and is one of a few wineries in the country to be able to do this.

A 15th Century Sussex barn on the farm is planned for restoration in the next year. This will be used to house a visitor centre and visitors will be able to taste the wines in a friendly and relaxed atmosphere. There are plans to organise a farm walk, including the ancient woodlands, wildflower meadows and the vineyard.

The priority at Davenport Vineyards will always be the production of their own wines from their own fruit. Davenport Vineyards have never purchased grapes to boost volumes of their own wines, believing that it is essential to control the grape growing in order to guarantee the best quality of wine. Davenport Vineyards have supported the English Quality Scheme since its first year, and are supporters of English Wine Producers, a national body set up to help the promotion of English wines.

In 2000 Will Davenport registered the vineyards at Horsmonden and Rotherfield with the Soil Association. Since then all grape growing and wine production has been fully organic although the wines will not be labelled as organic until the mandatory three-year conversion period is fulfilled. This has further boosted the sales of Davenport wines and also created more demand for advisory work from other vineyards. Will also writes a regular column for the UK Vineyards Association magazine on organic growing and winemaking. He was one of two main speakers at the UKVA symposium in December 2001 and he is generally considered to be one of the most knowledgeable people working in the UK with organic vines.

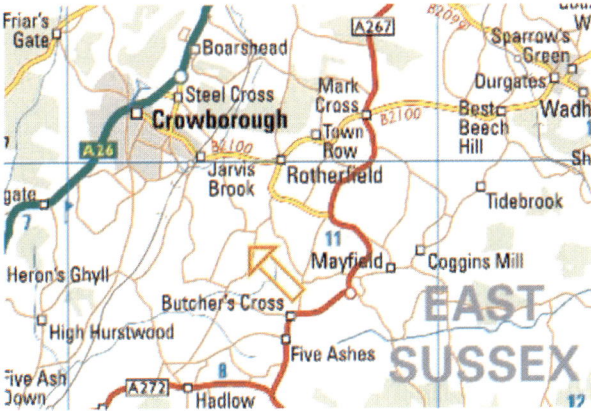

Denbies Wine Estate

Nestling in the beautiful Surrey hills just outside Dorking is one of the most marvellous and unexpected landscapes in England. With 265 acres under vine, Denbies is the largest privately owned vineyard in Northern Europe. Open all year, a multitude of facilities are available to visitors from vineyard and winery tours to wining and dining. Entrance to the estate and the chateau-style visitor centre is free.

Wine tasting tours operate hourly and include a 360 degree cinema bringing the vineyard cycle vividly to life, a trip through the winery aboard indoor "people movers" and the advice of an expert guide in tasting three selected wines.

You can walk the vineyard trails or go by train from April to November.

Fabulous food and surroundings, conservatory restaurant, panoramic wine bar, award winning wines, breath taking views across the beautiful Surrey Hills and a relaxed holiday ambience are just a few of the reasons to visit.

Stylish bed and breakfast accommodation is available at the original farmhouse.

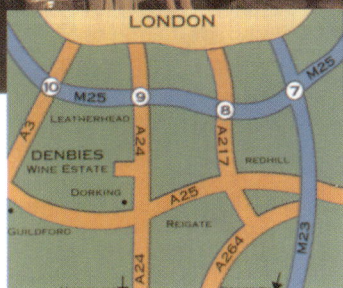

79

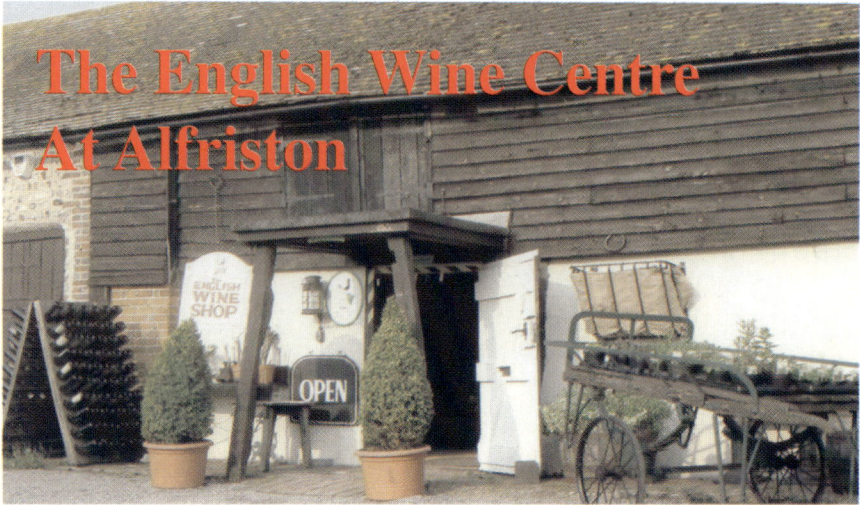

The English Wine Centre At Alfriston

I n 1967 Christopher and his brother Michael established The Valley Wine Cellars in the Cuckmere Valley outside the picturesque village of Alfriston, East Sussex. In 1972, under Christopher's management, it became The English Wine Centre and in the same year he planted the centre's experimental vineyard.

His main qualifications come from a passionate interest in wine and a first-hand experience of travelling, visiting vineyards and meeting vineyard proprietors in Europe and Australia.

With Michael he set up the hugely successful Frascos Wine Bar in Eastbourne - the second wine bar outside London - which reflected the revival of the UK's interest in wine.

"In the wine trade in the early '70s you had to specialize in an area or a region and since I was interested in regional food I thought that if I specialized in English wine I could use it as peg on which to promote regional food. The two things went together.

The wine trade was almost a closed shop in those days but because we bought a lot of wine for a very busy wine bar we found that we were establishing the volumes that allowed us to buy wine at a rate that enabled us to supply a range of wines to a developing group of friends. So by default we entered the wine trade.

The person who suggested making English wine to me had a very small vineyard just down the road from Alfriston on the South Downs. Vines seemed relatively easy to look after even though I discovered later that this wasn't the case and my small vineyard underwent a whole series of disasters. I wanted a vineyard of my own because I decided that if I was going to use English wine together with regional food then I needed to understand the product."

A Distinction in The Wine and Spirit Education Trust Higher Certificate Course provided Christopher with the grounding to develop The English Wine Centre and he started to run informal, informative and entertaining wine courses.

Tours, talks and tastings are now a major part of his business and Christopher is a leading expert on English wine, regularly contributing to radio and television programmes.

He launched the annual Alfriston English Wine and Regional Food Festival in 1975 and it is now the most important event of its type in the country. It became so successful that it outgrew the English Wine Centre and has now moved to a new venue.

"Very quickly one realized that there was a very real need to bring small wine producers together to give them a shop window and also to give them an ability to learn from what

Cuckmere English Wine in the cellars of the English Wine Centre.

neighbouring vineyards were doing - a little bit of industrial spying if you like. If one of the producers did very, very well at one of our Wine Festivals there had to be a reason - the product, the presentation, the labelling and so on and out of that competition developed.

At the same time the Festival has built up a loyalty around English wine among a group of people who like English wine and enjoy the ambience of the event. Over the years we've been amazed by how many people come back again and again bringing their families and friends.

I think marketing of English wine remains a problem because there are still people who haven't had any training in marketing. Some of the small vineyards maybe imagine that they can dip their toes in the water and that sales will develop without having given any real thought to how this is to be achieved.

A small vineyard with a single acre producing 1,000 bottles could probably dispose of them all within a radius of five miles but once you get to 10 or 20 acres the approach is going to have to be different altogether, something we can already see with the bigger vineyards. I think there will always be smaller vineyards and that many of them will continue to sell to loyal local followings, from the vineyard gate and at places like farmers' markets. Basically, vineyard owners are in four separate businesses, as a vine grower, as a wine maker, as a retailer and also in

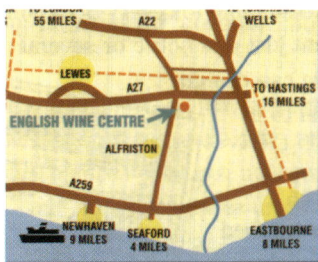

Barn Cottage, in the grounds of the English Wine Centre and available for lease.

the tourist industry and they have to decide how many they can take on at the same time. My feeling is that they should concentrate on grape growing or wine making and then decide how to market the wine. Its much better that we have big specialist producers with world wine making experience but there is still a place for small boutique vineyards like those in Australia or California which provide the interest for tourists.

Fortunately, for the size of our industry, we enjoy a disproportionate amount of very good media coverage and support from newspapers, magazines and the electronic media and this helps boost the visibility of English wine to the consumer."

In 1978 Christopher Ann was founder chairman of The Weald and Downland Vineyards Association. While serving on the association's board he took on responsibility for creating the corporate image of the national English Vineyards Association, including the English wine glass logo which is now readily recognised.

He created A Taste of Sussex in 1989. The non-profit marketing group set out to raise the profile of local produce, which includes a delicious range of wines, cheeses and dairy produce, cider, beer, soft drinks, ice cream, meat, fish, sauces, bread and bakery items. The organisation maintained a steady growth and is now under the umbrella of A Taste of the South East, which covers Sussex and Surrey.

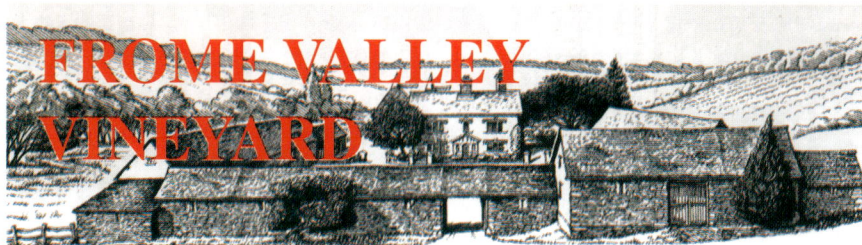

FROME VALLEY VINEYARD

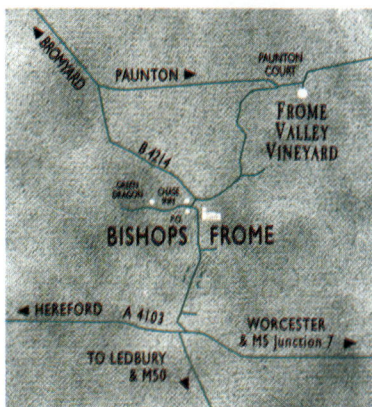

**Paunton Court,
Bishops Frome,
Herefordshire
WR6 5BJ
Tel: 01885 490735;
Fax 01885 490736.
e-mail
sales@fromewine.co.uk.**

Our vineyard of over four acres is situated on a gentle south-facing slope in rural Herefordshire which is protected from the North winds by an ancient damson hedge. We grow 90 percent white grapes, but have recently planted some black to make our popular dry rose wine. Our model demonstration vineyard is a feature where we show many varietals of vines, pruning and trellising methods. It is adjacent to our elegant tasting room which is in an antique threshing barn, where a selection of our wines are available for visitors to sample and to buy. We also stock a number of other local products such as cider, perry, beer, apple juice and honey.

Over the past few years we have won a number of awards for our wine in both regional and national competitions. Our Schonburger Quality Wine has twice won a silver cup for being the best dry white wine in competitions organised by the the South West Vineyard Association.

David Longman

This coming year we will be launching our sparkling wine under the name of Paunton Cremant and we are sure it will be another winner.

We welcome individual and group visitors, the latter preferably by appointment. We are open from the beginning of April to the end of October, on Wednesdays to Sundays and Bank Holiday Mondays from 11am to 5pm. We are always pleased to see people at other times by appointment. We make no charge to individual visitors, but a small one to groups, as this includes a full-guided tour and light refreshments after the tasting. We have disabled access to both the Tasting Room and the Model Vineyard.

For further information please contact David or Clare Longman or look at our web site: www.fromewine.co.uk

Hidden Spring Vineyard

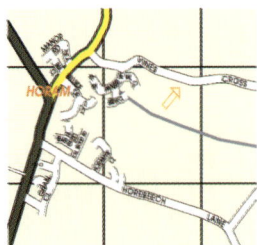

Vines Cross Road,
Horam,
Heathfield,
East Sussex TN21 OHE
Tel/Fax 01435 812640

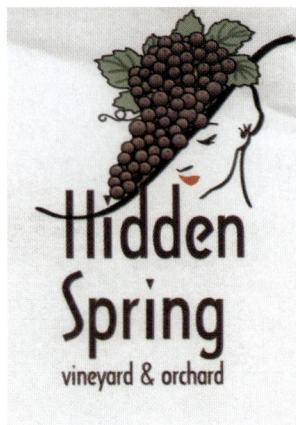

J ust outside Horam in East Sussex, on gentle south facing slopes, Hidden Springs Vineyard was established in 1987 with further plantings in 1988, adjoining a Soil Association approved organic orchard.

The grape varieiets are Ortega, Faber, Pinot Noir, Dunkelfelder, Muller Thurgau, Reichensteiner and Seyval Blanc.

Hidden Springs wines have achieved a high status receiving awards in both national and international competitions.

There is a vineyard shop where you can sample and buy the wines and after a tour of the vineyard you can enjoy a home made picnic hamper which includes a bottle of Hidden Springs Wine.

However, if you're planning to eat, do please book ahead.

WINE SELECTION

Fume - A careful blend of grapes producing a buttery dry white wine with complex fruit flavours, enhanced by the subtle use of oak. A clean and aromatic nose, soft melon fruit, crisp and zingy. This wine is own labelled for Fortnum & Mason as their English House wine, something that Hidden Spring is very proud to have been doing for some eight years. The 2000 vintage wine won the CLA (Country Land and Business Association) wine of the year award for 2001.

Decadence - A blend of Seyval Blanc and Faber. A touch of Noble Rot on Faber, a stopped fermentation and early bottling gave a slight spritz to this off-dry wine. Ideal with white meat, fish or an aperitif.

Sussex Sunset - Sussex Sunset is a blend of Pinot Noir, Ortega and Dunkelfelder. A fresh and fruity off-dry Rose which will complement picnics, salads, barbecues and Oriental cuisine. This wine has been consistently winning bronze medals in the International Wine Challenge over the past five years.

Dark Fields - Winner of the South East Wine of the Year 1998 and the Wine Guild Trophy 1998. An exceptional English Pinot Noir. Fermented and aged in new French barriques, exhibiting true Pinot Noir characteristics with silky smooth tannins, red berry fruit flavours and a hint of violets.

Hidden Spring Quality Vintage Brut - Made from selected grape varieties Pinot Noir, Faber and Seyval Blanc. Made in the traditional way fermented in the bottle, then allowing 18 months in the bottle before being released. This wine exhibits traditional yeasty characteristics with a gentle mousse and soft fruit style.

Organic Apple dry/Organic Sweet Surrender - These wonderfully refreshing apple wines are a blend of several varieties of our Soil Association Approved apples. Drink well chilled for a delicious taste experience. If it is a dryer wine you prefer, try Organic Apple dry but if you have a sweeter palate then Organic Sweet Surrender will be the one for you.

La Mare Vineyards

**St. Mary,
Jersey,
Channel Islands JE3 3BA
Tel:01534 481178
Fax: 01534 485210
tim@lamarejersey.com
W: www.lamarejersey.com
Contact: Tim Crowley
Managing Director**

La Mare has twenty one acres of vineyards, producing 40,000 bottles of wine per annum. The major grape varieties are Seyval Blanc, Phoenix, Reichensteiner, Huxelrebe, Pinot Noir, Regent and Rondo.

La Mare is lucky to have the skills of our Production Manager, Simon Day, formerly winemaker at Lamberhurst Vineyards in Kent, and Denbies Vineyard in Surrey. Coupled with extensive experience with Brown Brothers in Australia, Simon continues to develop the wine and brandy side of La Mare, with new techniques and several new wines.

The La Mare visitor centre is open from Easter to October, offering tours of the vineyards, winery and distillery, tastings of all their products, audio-visual show, cooperage, tea rooms and well stocked shop. Conference facilities and events are also offered for groups of 10 - 800!

LA MARE WINES

Cuvee de La Mare
Made using the traditional method of bottle fermentation as in Champagne,

using ripe Pinot Blanc and Seyval Blanc grapes aged on its yeast lees for well over nine months before disgorgement. The resultant wine is Brut, with a light floral quality, creamy fruit, beautifully clean elegant palate and a wonderful, mouth filling fizz! Winner of a silver medal at the International Wine and Spirit Competition 2001.

Lillie

This Brut traditional method sparkling wine is made using Pinot Noir and Triomphe. Fantastic aromas with cherries and elderberry on the nose and a full fruity palate, with a hint of sloes. The mousse is fine and mouth filling, with a long pleasing finish. Bronze medal winner at the IWSC in 2001

Domaine De La Mare

Made using a blend of Seyval Blanc and Phoenix, Domaine has undergone fermentation in French oak barriques. Lees stirring over six months and a softening malo-lactic fermentation, make a complex wine of great length and character. The wine has just a hint of oak character, with grapefruit, lime and a subtle herbaceous aroma, integrating well with the soft buttery vanilla flavours.

Clos De La Mare

Clos combines Reichensteiner, Huxelrebe, and Schonburger grapes to give a fresh, crisp and fruity wine. Jersey sunshine provides high quality ripe grapes with good flavour development and this reflects well in the finished wine. Fermented cool in stainless steel vats, the wine has minimal handling and is bottled young to retain freshness and varietal characteristics. The wine is off dry, with the slight sweetness balancing the crisp acidity. Bronze medal winner IWSC 2001.

Jersey Grapple

This luscious fruit wine is made with a blend of grape wine and cider. This unusual wine was first created in Elizabethan times, when galleons bringing casks of wine from Spain and the south of France to England, docked in Jersey for supplies. During the long voyage, the casks would lose wine (evaporation or a thirsty crew!) and Jersey cider was used to top up the casks and then resealed for shipment to England! La Mare's version has refreshing spicy apple aromas, ripe grapey flavours, and a crisp sweetness that lingers on the tongue.

The Jersey Distillery at La Mare

The first brandy still since the 1800's is now installed at La Mare and is producing Jersey Apple Brandy.

La Mare Preserve Range

Using traditional recipes La Mare has built up the widest and best known range of locally produced preserves on the island. Favourites include Whisky Marmalade, Apricot Jam with Rum, Wine Mustard and these have now been joined by Jersey Cream Fudge and Jersey Apple Brandy Fudge and the Jersey speciality of Black Butter - a dark preserve made using apples, liquorice and spices.

UK wines are on sale at London's Thames-side Vinopolis wine tasting and wine retail centre and UK wine calendar events are held there.

Meopham Valley Vineyard

Norway House,
Wrotham Road,
Meopham
DA13 OAU
Tel and fax: 01474
812727

Meopham Valley Vineyard is unusual in that no chemicals are used to protect the vines or improve the soil other than those authorized by the Soil Association.

Owner, David Grey, says that from the day the vineyard was first planted in 1991 he and his wife, Pauline, didn't feel right about pouring "loads of noxious chemicals" onto the field or the vines.

At a time when consumers are increasingly concerned about the use of chemicals in food and drinks, a handful of organic vineyards have appeared in UK viticulture.

Nevertheless, to combat mildew and fungus, Meopham does spray with sulphur and copper and is unusually vigilant in ensuring that the flow of air around grapes is particularly good.

Grape varieties include Chardonnay, Pinot Noir, Pinot Gris, Madeleine Angevine, Reichensteiner, Triomphe and Leon Millot.

The two hectare vineyard grows a substantial range of grapes and makes white, red, rose and sparkling wines.

It was planted after David and his wife discovered how

much they enjoyed visiting vineyards. They had visited some in France but concluded that finding suitable land in England would be easier.

David and Pauline set up Meopham Vineyard with the advice of Gillian Pearkes, an authority on grape growing in England who gave courses in Devon.

Some of their grapes are sold to other vineyards but those used in their own wines are sold from the vineyard shop, by all accounts an Aladdin's cave of fascination and choice.

Buying wine for those who don't know much about grapes can be challenging but David and Pauline make a point of welcoming clients visiting Meopham to taste any of their wines - without obligation. Groups are also catered to with a tour of the vineyard and a tasting of six wines en route around the vines.

Visitors to Meopham enjoy a friendly and highly personal service from a couple who chose to grow grapes and sell wine because they love doing it.

"We hope more people will come to Meopham to have a look

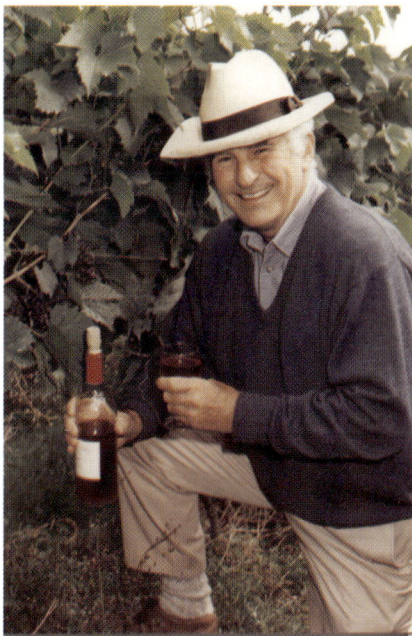

David Grey

around, have a good time and, hopefully, buy some wine."

Situated at Wrotham, Kent, Meopham Valley Vineyard produces white, red, rose and sparkling wines

Her Majesty, the Queen and the Duke Of Edinburgh toast the City of London in wine from Nutbourne Vineyards at a lunch at London's Guildhall to mark the Royal couple's Golden Wedding Anniversary in November 1997. To the Queen's left is the Lord Mayor of the City of London, Richard Nichols DCL and to the Duke's right, Lady Nichols.

94

New Wave Wines' latest range of Curious Grape wines

RidgeView Wine Estate

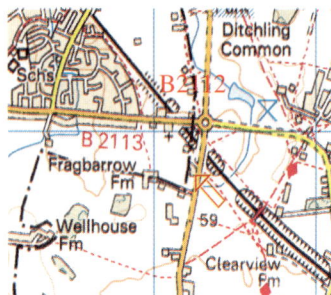

**Fragbarrow Lane,
Ditchling Common,
Hassocks,
East Sussex BN6 8TP.
Tel: 01444 258039.
Fax: 01444 230757**

RidgeView Estate is dedicated to making high quality sparkling wine, employing traditional methods and growing the same grape varieties as used in France: Chardonnay for backbone and finesse, Pimot Meunier for richness of fruit and Pinot Noir for body and depth. Ridgeview's wine, Cuvee Merret® - named as a tribute to Englishman Christopher Merret who first recorded sparkling wine in London in the 1600s - is bottle fermented in cellars where the

cool even temperature encourages a fine mousse and provides ideal conditions for ageing.

RidgeView's Bloomsbury 1996 won the International Wine Competition Trophy for best English Wine as well as the United Kingdom Vineyard Association national trophies for best wine. Winners of nine medals in international competition. The wines are sold nationally through The Sunday Times Wine Club, Laithwaites and Waitrose as well as through twenty independent resellers. The estate also delivers by mail order anywhere in the UK.

PROUD

Our embassy in Paris is host to millions of foreign guests and dignitaries each year. Always proud to promote and show off the quality of British products, the Ambassador, Sir John Holmes, has selected RidgeView's international award winning sparkling wine Cuvee Merret Bloomsbury to give to his guests.

Mike Roberts, a director and wine maker at the Sussex vineyard and winery says: " I am extremely proud and pleased to have been selected by such a prestigious embassy. The charge d'affairs, Commander Allan Adare told me that in the past the Embassy has always presented the Champagne Pol Roger to their visitors because of its association with Sir Winston Churchill. But now, the Embassy can be confident in showing off an exceptional English wine to their guests."

97

Rossiters Vineyard

Situated at Wellow, Yarmouth, Isle of Wight, Rossiters Vineyard produces red and white wines.

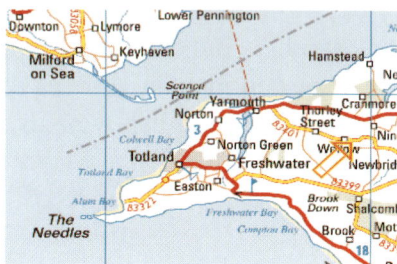

**Rossiters Farmhouse,
Wellow,
Yarmouth, P041 0TE
Isle of Wight.
Tel: 01983 761138.
Fax: 01983 760263**

Professor Rod Thompson succumbed to the lure of viticulture after a decade as a Fellow and eventually director of medical studies at Corpus Christi College, Cambridge University. He accepted a chair at Southampton University but decided to base himself on the Isle of Wight, where he had enjoyed living as a teenager. A fast hydrofoil service allowed him to commute coast to coast in twenty minutes, keeping a car parked at both ends of the journey.

He was lucky enough to be able to purchase a small property near Yarmouth which came with fifteen acres of land. Rod knew nothing about farming but soon began wondering to what use he could put his newly acquired acres, including a five acre south facing slope. He soon realized that grapes were being grown in the island's hospitable climate giving him the idea to try his hand at wine making.

"It was an ideal site and planting vines seemed a great deal more romantic than anything else. There's something intensely satisfying about wandering about your own vineyard on a summer's evening. And you have a feeling of being part of a very ancient tradition. In September and October the vines are groaning with grapes; the red ones look very dark and beautiful. Then the leaves start turning red. At harvest time about 20 people come to help pick the grapes, some of them bringing

children and even their dogs. We have have lunch by the side of the barn and drink some wine and then pick some more. It's great fun."

Rod Thompson's Rossiters Vineyard is situated in the western part of the Isle of Wight which with its mild climate and long hours of sunshine provides a highly favourable location for planting vines. Back in 1990, the south facing slope was first divided in half by planting a hedge of native English species - hazel, hawthorne, dogwood, hornbeam and wild maple and one half of the field planted with approximately 3,000 vines. This took about eight days and as the last vine went in, following a rain shower, a rainbow appeared, augering well for the vineyard's future.

"The first vines were a mixture of Seyval Blanc and Madeleine Angevine - the former definitely of French origin and the latter probably so. Then Regner, Reichensteiner and Schonburger were planted - all of German origin. Schonburger is a delightful grape which, although a white wine variety, turns blush pink as it ripens and can easily be used as a table grape. At the time of this first planting, a few rows of a new variety, Orion, were included. This again was bred in Germany and was reputed to produce a wine indistinguishable from Reisling.

In 1990, there was still doubt as to whether it was possible to produce a decent English red wine. (These doubts have now been dispelled and vine varieties producing red wine have increased enormously since then). During our first planting, two rows of Dornfelder - a German red wine grape - and one row of Dunkelfelder (again German) were planted. The latter is used not really because it produces wine but because it imparts a deep red colour when blended with other wine varieties. Finally, we planted three rows of a grape which then had a 'Gm' number but was afterwards called Amurensis. Germany has several excellent viticulture institutes breeding and testing new wine varieties. Of these, perhaps the most famous is Geisenheim, hence the Gm number. The original Amurensis vine was discovered on the Chinese-Russian border, where the summers are short and the winters are hard - hence the vine has to ripen quickly or else. This variety does well in the English climate. In 1996, a Rossiters red wine produced from these varieties won a silver medal in the Wessex Vineyards Association Wine of the Year Competition.

In 1992-94, the other half of the five acre field was planted with a similar number of vines, a mixture of Orion, Reichensteiner and Seyval Blanc in equal proportions. In 1998, an adjacent beautifully sheltered meadow was purchased and planted with about 3,000 Bacchus and 1,000 Rondo vines. Bacchus was again bred in Germany and is a white wine variety gaining increasing popularity in the United Kingdom. Rondo is a red wine variety which has supplanted Amurensis although it has Amurensis in its parentage.

The winery and bottle store at Rossiters is a barn which began life many years ago as a pig sty, then it became a chicken farm and finally a barn for storing farm equipment. This has been converted to contain a Vaslin screw press and several 850L stainless steel ex-brewery tanks, all purchased second hand. Fermentation usually lasts six weeks. The wine is then 'racked,' i.e. the sediment pumped off about three times at monthly intervals. It usually clears on its own (the barn is fairly cool) and is bottled by May.

One of the biggest challenges in running a vineyard is marketing the product. At the moment, the outlets are local shops and hotels and as yet sales are not made to the mainland. The population of the Isle of Wight is about 129,000. However, there are two-and-a-half million tourists visiting the island every year who clearly need to be targeted!

Rossiters Vineyard sells a white wine which is a judicious blend of the white wine varieties described above and also a red wine which is a blend of the red varieties."

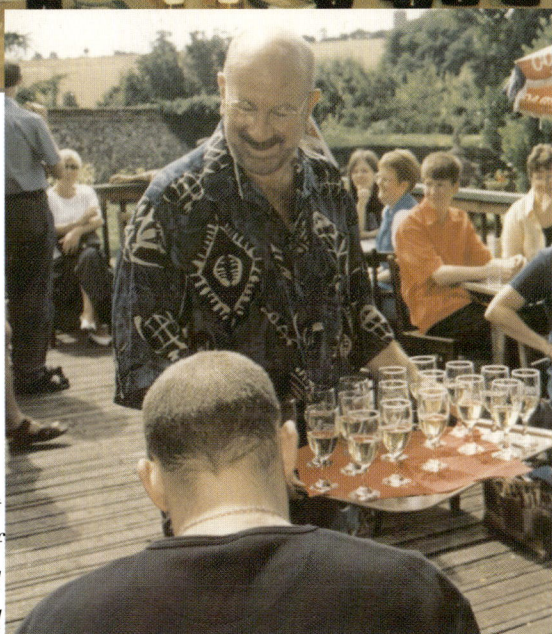

Picture on the right courtesey of Chilford Hall Vineyard

Sherborne Castle Estates

S elf evidently, this vineyard is part of Sherborne Castle Estates.

English wines have a clean, crisp fragrance and a delicate fruitiness that is unique and unmatched by wines from warmer climates.

The Sherborne Castle Estate Vineyard is a perfect example of an English vineyard producing fine English wines.

These wines can be purchased from Sherborne Castle shop by the bottle or by the case.

Opening times 31st March to 31st October
Castle, Gardens, Shop and Tearoom - open every day, except Mondays and Fridays (but open on Bank Holiday Mondays) from 11.00 am with last admission at 4.30 pm.
Castle opens on Saturdays from 2.30pm with last admission at 4.30 pm
Up to 4 children admitted free, accompanied by paying adult

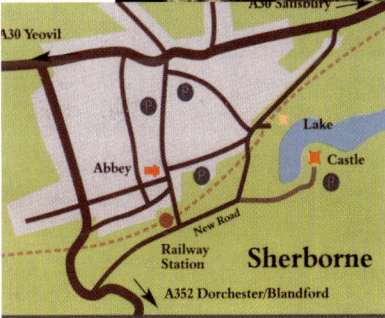

**Sherborne Castle,
Sherborne,
Dorset DT9 3PY**

www.sherbornecastle.com enquiries@sherbornecastle.com

Three Choirs Vineyards

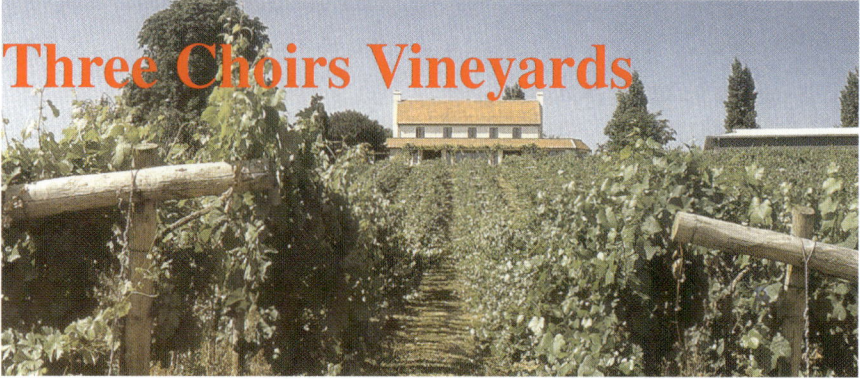

The Key To Marketing English Wine Is Having A Product That People Want

Three Choirs Vineyards have been growing grapes and making wines for 26 years. It began with half an acre and today farms 75 acres of vines at Newent in Gloucestershire selling approximately 250,000 to 300,000 bottles of English wine each year. The site is beautiful and a wine shop, a la carte restaurant and luxurious accommodation have been put in place to attract wine lovers and even tourists. I went there to talk to Managing Director, Thomas Shaw.

Three Choirs has a reputation as a successful marketer. What is required to successfully market UK wine?

The most important thing is to produce wines that

people want. We have always produced a range of wines right the way through the spectrum of dry wines, oaked, non-oaked through to sweeter wines, sparkling, red and rose and the public like that. People will find something in the Three Choirs range that they like to drink.

Is there any degree of consumer resistance to buying UK wine?

Consumer resistance is still a factor but there are also people who say that they don't want Eastern European wines even though there are very good ones available. It takes time for people to get to know wines. People around the world are drinking more wine and trying more wines and that helps English wine.

Are UK wines visible in the market place?

English wines are not hugely visible but the reason is that the quantities produced are still small. We've overcome this problem by attracting people to visit the vineyard. They leave here knowing about English wine and later on they look for it on their supermarket shelves. Most major supermarkets stock our wines. The more unusual varietals are sold exclusively from the vineyard but people order and have them delivered to their homes.

Are people sufficiently familiar with the grapes used in making English wine?

Some are but I would say that the variety names are not so important in English wines. A few stand out. For example, Bacchus is reasonably well known but otherwise the names the public know are quite limited. Most people are put off by a lot of the Germanic sounding names because they think they're going to be given piesporter or liebfraumilch. Three Choirs' wines have been given generic names that the public can pronounce easily and can remember.

So how do UK consumers choose English wine?

The most important thing with English wine is getting people to taste it; then they're happy. Certainly many more people have tasted English wine today than five years ago. Those who say they don't know that wine is made in the UK and haven't tried it are very few in number.

Has Three Choirs changed its marketing policy because of the public attitude to grape varietals?

Yes, we have. We used to emphasize promoting the varietal names and we still do for our customers who visit the shop and want to learn more about English wine. But in supermarkets we decided to give a generic names to our wines with details provided on the back label. Labels are very important because consumers certainly want to know about taste and sweetness and to be reassured that some effort has been put into the production.

Do supermarkets provide the space that UK wine vendors need?

Yes, we're selling all the wine we can produce. I think the supermarkets are doing as much as they can although it might be nice if sometimes they would do a little more to promote English wines - shelf signs, for example, instead of lumping us in with the rest of the world.

If more consumers buy English wine how will the upsurge in demand be met?

There are more vineyards than ever today particularly as people have opened vineyards as a kind of lifestyle statement. The problems come when they try to sell the wine because you've either got to find a supermarket or find ways of reaching the public. Then its not lifestyle; it's a business. When people first plant vines they don't think about marketing wine because it seems far into the future. When the time comes, for some of them, it's a nightmare because they really don't want to go out and market.

There are people who grow and sell to the bigger vineyards and that's always a possibility because the money needed for presses and tanks is considerable. Three Choirs produces wine for between twenty and twenty five other vineyards. I think we will see more acreage in the future and there is certainly a place for other good producers but just how the industry will develop is difficult to forecast.

How interested are people in visiting the vineyard?

Some are very interested while others who come have absolutely no idea how grapes are grown but the vineyards are very beautiful and attractive to walk. People who enjoy and are interested in wine have a very good experience here. The vast majority want to come and taste English wine but there are those who are very interested in seeing how the grapes are grown and how the wine is made. We show them a video and they can taste the wines and look round the vineyard with the aid of one of our guidebooks which is available in the shop. We also have accommodation here and majority of guests stay because of its quality. The rooms are very comfortable with lots of space and beautiful views. People come for many different reasons; some people love wine, others come because they know they're going to get peace and quiet in the vineyard and some don't drink wine at all; they just like the place. There are very few places in this country with such a beautiful setting and good food, too. In fact, the vineyard is so attractive that we even offer art courses here.

For the smaller producers who want to sell their own wine I think the only way is from the vineyard and so the owner has to do something to make people want to go there. Our restaurant and accommodation are extras we offer combined with our special events programme but everyone has to think of something similar to attract consumers. You can never do enough. If more vineyards think about tourism then vineyards tours and wine breaks will certainly increase. They are possible now. It's up to the vineyard owners to do more to develop vineyard tourism. In our case we'll soon open a micro-brewery on site where we'll be brewing our own beer. It's just another way of attracting people to the site. Those who don't want to drink wine will have the choice of drinking beer.

We are using our vineyard facilities to the full by offering special dinner programmes sometimes including live music, summer BBQs and festival wine and dine programmes. There is even a murder mystery dinner. We cater to private and corporate groups and not only to individuals.

How do you promote Three Choirs so that the public know about you?

Word of mouth. Personal recommendation is by far the strongest way but the Internet is also getting better and better. People are beginning to realize that there are vineyards in England and when they go on holiday they look for them. But you've always got to market and the key is to identify where the public are most likely to look - Internet, supermarkets, tourist information centres. Whatever vineyards choose to do to promote themselves has to be done properly and professionally. For example, if they want to be open to visitors they have to be open when visitors want to come, to be open and friendly and happy to let people taste their wines. But as I said at the beginning the most important factor of all is making a product that the public want. If whatever you do is done well word of mouth will do the rest.

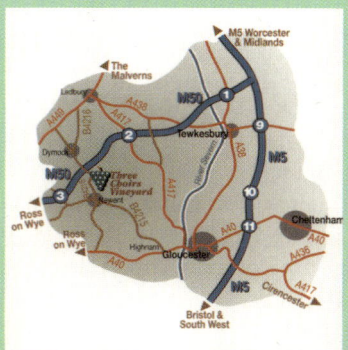

Windmill Vineyard

Hellidon, Northamptonshire
Telephone 01327 262023

The vineyards produces red and white wines from grapes grown on site and country wines produced from fruit grown on our own farm or picked from hedgerows. Our list includes Sloe, Elderberry, Blackberry, Damson Silver Birch, Quince, Cherry and many others. We conduct guided tours for visitors every weekend from Easter until October or at other times by appointment.

Seyval Blanc
English Table Wine

1998

75 cl e   Dry   alc 10 %
Bottled by Windmill Vineyard
Hellidon, Northamptonshire
wm   *Producer of England*

Selected Vineyards Across The UK

Adgestone Vineyard,
Sandown,
Isle of Wight PO36 OES

Astley Vineyards,
Stourport-On-Severn,
Worcestershire DY13 ORU

Avalon Vineyard,
East Pennard,
Shepton Mallet,
Somerset BA4 6UY

Bagborough Vineyard,
Pylle,
Shepton Mallet,
Somerset BA4 6SX

Bardfield Vineyard,
Great Bardfield,
Braintree,
Essex CM7 4QD

Barnsgate Vineyard,
Herons Ghyll,
Near Uckfield,
East Sussex TN22 4DB

Battle Wine Estate,
Leeford Vineyard,
Whatlington,
Battle,
East Sussex TN33 OND

Bearsted Vineyard,
Maidstone,
Kent.

Biddenden Vineyard,
Little Whatmans,
Biddenden,
Ashford,
Kent TN27 8DH

Blackwater Valley Vineyard,
Tirraun,
Gortnagross,
Mallow,
County Cork,
Republic of Ireland

Bodenham English Wines,
Broadfield Court Estate,
Bodenham,
Herefordshire HR1 3LG

Bothy Vineyard,
Frilford Heath,
Abingdon OX13 6QW,
Oxfordshire

Bow In The Cloud Vineyard,
Garsden,
Malmesbury,
Wiltshire

Boze Down Vineyard,
Whitchurch-On-Thames,
Reading,
Oxfordshire RG8 7QS

Bookers Vineyard,
Bolney,
West Sussex RH17 5NB

Breaky Bottom Vineyard,
Rodmell,
Lewes,
East Sussex Bn7 3EX.

Broxbournebury Vineyard,
Palmers Green,
London N13 5PG

Bruisyard Vineyard,
Saxmondham,
Suffolk.

Burwash Weald Vineyard,
Etchingham,
East Sussex TN19 7LA

Camel Valley Vineyard,
Nanstallon,
Bodmin,
Cornwall.

Chanctonbury Vineyard,
Wiston,
West Sussex RH20 3DF

Clawford Vineyard,
Holsworthy,
Devon EX22 6PN

Coach House Vineyard,

West Wellow,
Romsey,
Hampshire SO51 6BW

Compton Green Vineyard,
Maxstoke,
Aston Ingham,
Ross On Wye,
Herefordshire HR9 7LS

Conghurst Vineyard,
Hawkhurst,
Kent TN18 4RW

Court Lane Vineyard,
Ropley,
Alresford,
Hampshire SO24 ODE.

Cheddar Valley Vineyard,
Axbridge,
Somerset BS26 2AN

Clay Hill Vineyard,
Lamberhurst,
Kent TN3 8LT

Dunkery Vineyard,
Wootton Courteney,
Minehead,
Devon.

Eglantine Vineyard,
Costock,
Loughborough,
Notinghamshire LE12 6UX

Elham Valley Vineyard,
Breach,
Barham,
Canterbury,
Kent CT4 6LN

Elms Cross Vineyard,
Bradford On Avon,
Wiltshire BA15 2AL

Eryri Vineyard,
Llanbedr,
Gwynedd,
Wales LL45 2DZ

Felsted Vineyard
Crix Green,
Felsted,
Great Dunmow,
Essex CM6 3JT

Fynnon Las Vineyard,
Aberaeron,
Dyfed,
Wales SA46 OED

Godstone Vineyard,
Surrey RH9 8DE.

Great Stocks Vineyard,

Stock,
Ingatestone,
Essex CM4 9RB

Hadlow Down Vineyard,
East Sussex TN22 4ET

Hagley Court Vineyard,
Bartestree,
Hereford HR1 4BX

Hale Valley Vineyard,
Boddington East,
Wendover,
Buckinghamshire HP22 6NQ

Halfpenny Green Vineyard,
Staffordshire DY7 5EP

Harden Vineyard,
Penshurst,
Near Tonbridge,
Kent TN11 8DX

Hazel End Vineyard,
Bishop's Stortford,
Hertfordshire CM23 1IG

Hendred Vineyard,
Ludbridge,
East Hendred,
Oxfordshire OX12 8HR

Horton Estate Vineyard,
Wimborne,
Dorset BH21 7JG

Ickworth Vineyard,
Hollinger,
Bury St. Edmunds,

Suffolk.

Iron Railway Vineyard,
Caulston
Surrey CR5 3DH.

Jays Farm Vineyard,
East Wellow,
Hampshire SO51 6DN

Leeds CastleVineyard,
Maidstone,
Kent ME17 IPL
Tel; 01622 765400
email: enquiries@leeds-castle.co.uk
Web: www.leeds-castle.com
Description: DRY, WHITE, CRISP
AND REFRESHING

Leventhorpe Vineyard,
Woodlesford,
Leeds,
West Yorkshire.

Lillibrooke Manor Vineyard,
Cox Green,
Maidenhead,
Berkshire SL6 3LP

Little Ashley Vineyard,
Bradford On Avon,
Wiltshire BA15 2PW

Little Foxes Vineyard,
Stonehouse,
Gloucestershire GL10 2HB

Llanerch Vineyard
Hensol,
Pendoylan,

Vale of Glamorgan,
Wales.

Manstree Vineyard,
Shillingford St. George,
Exeter,
Devon.

Mersea Vineyard,
East Mersea,
Colchester,
Essex CM5 9HF.

Mimram Valley Vineyard,
Tewin Water,
Welwyn,
Hertfordshire AL6 OAB

Monnow Valley Vineyard,
Monmouth,
Monmouthshire,
Wales NP25 4DL

Moorlynch Vineyard,
Bridgwater,
Somerset TA7 9DD

Morton Manor Vineyard,
Brading,
Isle of Wight.

Mumfords Vineyard,
Bannerdown,
Bath,
Somerset BA1 7LQ.

New Hall Vineyards,
Purleigh,
Chelmsford,
Essex.

Northbrook Springs Vineyard,
Bishop's Waltham,
Southampton,
Hampshire SO32 1FB.

Nyetimber Vineyard,
West Chiltington,
West Sussex RH20 2HH

Oakford Vineyard,
Bampton,
Devon EX16 9EW.

Offa's Vineyard - Peter Johnson,
The Old Rectory,
Llanvihangel-Ystern-Llewern,
Monmouthshire, NP25 5H1
Tel: 01600 780241
email: OFFA.VINES@VIRGIN.NET
White, Red, Sparkling

Old Forge Vineyard,
Fawley,
Near Henley,
Oxfordshire.

Parhams Vineyard,
Melbury Abbas,
Shaftsbury,
Dorset SP7 ODE

Penshurst Vineyards,
Tonbridge,
Kent TN11 8DU.

Polmassick Vineyard,
St. Ewe,
St. Austell,
Cornwall PL26 6HA.

Porthallow Vineyard,
St. Keverne,
Helston,
Cornwall TR12 6QH

Rodney Stoke Vineyard,
Clifton,
Bristol BS8 1HA

Rosemary Vinyard,
Ryde,
Isle of Wight PO33 2UX

Rowenden Vineyard,
Cranbrook,
Kent TN17 4PQ

Saint Anne's Vineyard
Oxenhall,
Newent,
Gloucestershire GL18 IRW

Saint Augustines Vineyard,
Aust,
South Glocestershire BS35 4BG

Sedlescombe Organic Vineyard,
Robertsbridge,
East Sussex TN32 5SA.

Sharphams Vineyard,
Ashprington,
Totnes,
Devon TQ9 7UT

Shawsgate Vineyard,
Framlinham,
Woodbridge,
Suffolk IP13 9HZ
Spring Barn Vineyard,

Laughton,
Near Lewes,
East Sussex BN8 6AN

Standen Vineyard,
East Grinstead,
West Sussex RH19 4NE.

Staple St James Winery,
Canterbury,
Kent CT3 1LN

Staverton Vineyard,
Eyke,
Woodbridge,
Suffolk IP12 2RR

Sun Vineyard,
Bellingdon,
Near Chesham,
Buckinghamshire HP22 2XW

Surrenden Vineyard,
 Walnut Tree Farm,
Swan lane,
Little Chart,
Nr. Ashford,
Kent TN27 OPS.
Tel: 01233-840214
Fax: 01233 840703
email: martin@e-mould.net
SPARKLING (Chardonnay, Pinot
Noir, Pinot Meunier) only made
by FCC, Twyford
(Four Corners Consultancy -
John Worontschek)
Limited supply.

Thames Valley Vineyards,
Stanlake Park,
Twyford, Reading,
Berkshire.

Thorncroft Vineyard,
Leatherhead,
Surrey KT22 8JD

Tiltridge Vineyard,
Upton Upon Severn,
Worcestershire WR8 OSA

Tintern Vineyard,
Near Chepstow,
Monmouthshire,
Wales NP16 6S

Welland Valley Vineyard,
Marsden Trussell,
Market Harborough,
Leicestershire LE16 9TX.

West Stoke House Vineyard,
Chichester,
West Sussex PO18 9BN
Wickham Vineyard,
Shedfield,Southampton,
Hampshire.

Wroxeter Roman Vineyard,
Shrewsbury,
Shropshire SY5 6PQ

Wylye Valley Vineyard,
Warminster,
Wiltshire.

NOTES

*Label from
Hidden Springs
Vineyard*

Gateway Books

Gateway Books is an imprint familiar in Singapore, Indonesia and Malaysia for 20 years but British born owner Richard Mann is only now publishing books about the UK. Mann is especially interested in titles reflecting change dynamics in the UK as well as in UK heritage tourism.

After gaining a degree in international politics and economics at York University, Richard Mann began his career in UK daily newspapers moving to the Far East in the 1970s where he joined the Hong Kong Government Information Services Department. There he headed up the Hong Kong International Arts Festival Press Unit and eventually became Head of the Government Secretariat Press Office.

With the appearance of personal computers in the early 1980s he moved to North America to edit consumer computer publications.

Gateway Books began by publishing titles of interest to the flood of Chinese immigrants out of Hong Kong in the run up to 1997, heading largely to Canada, Australia and New Zealand. Subsequently Gateway rode the Southeast Asian economic boom of the 1990s with business titles of interest to foreigners investing or buying and selling in the region.